SCHOLASTIC

Quick & Easy Math Art

Deborah Schecter

NEW YORK • TORONTO • LONDON • AUCKLAND • SYDNEY
MEXICO CITY • NEW DELHI • HONG KONG • BUENOS AIRES

Teaching *Resources*

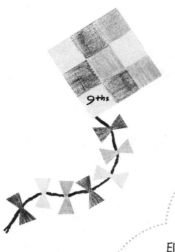

Special thanks to Robert Krech,
Elementary Math Curriculum Specialist,
West Windsor-Plainsboro School District,
Princeton Junction, New Jersey,
and to editor Mackie Rhodes—
for their invaluable help with this book.

Scholastic Inc. grants teachers permission to photocopy the reproducible pages from this book for classroom use. No other part of this publication may be reproduced in whole or in part, or stored in a retrieval system, or transmitted in any form or by any means, electronic, mechanical, photocopying, recording, or otherwise, without written permission of the publisher. For information regarding permission, write to Scholastic Inc., 557 Broadway, New York, NY 10012.

"Rainbow Bead Rulers" activity adapted from *Hello Kitty Beads Activity Book* by Kris Hirschmann.
Copyright © 2002 by Scholastic Inc. Used with permission of the publisher.

Angle Tester idea adapted from *The Great Big Book of Super-Fun Math Activities*.
Copyright © 1999 by Scholastic Inc. Used with permission of the publisher.

Cover design: Maria Lilja
Interior design: Kathy Massaro
Interior illustrations: Jo Lynn Alcorn, Maxie Chambliss, Kate Flanagan, and James Graham Hale
Interior photographs: Helen Pavlac

Text copyright © 2011 by Deborah Schecter
Illustrations and photographs copyright © 2011 by Scholastic Inc.
ISBN: 978-0-439-19942-1
Published by Scholastic Inc.
All rights reserved.
Printed in the U.S.A.

Contents

About This Book

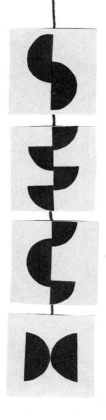

Welcome to *Quick & Easy Math Art*. The activities and projects in this book are designed to help you connect math and art in your classroom. Each activity is both a hands-on math exploration and an art experience that will naturally appeal to a range of learning styles. As students create delightful and dazzling art projects, math concepts will become concrete and meaningful, and they'll have opportunities to problem solve and practice skills in number sense, place value, multiplication, division, fractions, algebra, geometry, measurement, data analysis, and much more.

You can use the activities and projects to introduce or review math concepts, to culminate particular math units you are teaching, or simply to introduce an art experience. And many projects connect with seasonal celebrations and other special holidays throughout the year. Using easy-to-find materials, students can create beautiful gifts and decorations for family and friends—and deepen their understanding of math concepts at the same time.

Each lesson includes a photo that shows how a sample completed project looks, a detailed list of all materials and equipment needed, step-by-step directions with supportive illustrations, and teaching and management tips to help projects go smoothly. Many lessons also include reproducible patterns, student record sheets, and Explore More ideas—suggestions for extending the math concept or varying the basic project.

Meeting the Math Standards

The lessons and activities in this book are designed to support you in meeting the content and process standards outlined by the National Council of Teachers of Mathematics (NCTM) in its *Principles and Standards for School Mathematics* (2000). See the skills matrix, page 6, for more.

The activities also correlate with the math standards recommended by the Common Core State Standards Initiative, a state-led effort to establish a single set of clear educational standards aimed at providing students with a high-quality education. At the time this book went to press, these standards were in the process of being finalized. To learn more, go to www.corestandards.org.

Tips for Success

* Most of the projects use materials that are low cost and easy to collect. Many use items you can recycle, such as old file folders, cardboard, copy paper, gift wrap, and egg cartons. Save scraps of construction paper, bits of felt, yarn and ribbons—all of these will come in handy.

* Try to test each project before doing it with students. This will help you identify needed materials and assess the amount of time you'll need, including time for setup and cleanup. Doing the project yourself will also help you prepare to guide students through the project. You can use your completed project as an example when you introduce the activity to students.

* To make the setup, distribution, and cleanup go smoothly, organize materials in labeled containers on a table. Have trays available to students for collecting materials. (Copy-paper box lids work well.)

* If time is short, consider spreading some activities over several days, or inviting students to take their projects home to finish with a family member. You'll find that many projects are suitable for learning-center setups, too, allowing students to help one another and share ideas. Stock the center with the necessary materials, post directions, and review the steps of the activity with students ahead of time. If activities include introductory discussions of math concepts, plan to do these with the class before having students work on their own at the center.

* Allow plenty of time for students to think and to ask questions. Encourage them to share observations, tips, problems, and solutions with classmates as they work. To wrap up an activity, bring students together for a discussion, and invite them to share their creations and discoveries with the class.

A Note About Safety

The projects in this book use materials that are safe for students to handle. However, adult supervision is recommended for all projects. When sending activities home, include a note suggesting that an adult family member do the activity with the student.

Connections With the Math Standards

The matrix below shows how the lessons and activities in this book correlate with the content and process skill standards recommended by NCTM. Specific topics within each standard are listed at the beginning of each lesson.

	Number & Operations	Algebra	Geometry	Measurement	Data Analysis & Probability	Problem Solving	Reasoning & Proof	Communication	Connections	Representation
100-Quill Critters	*					*	*	*	*	*
Picture-a-Number Posters	*		*		*	*	*	*	*	*
Place Value Speedway	*					*	*	*	*	*
Gingerbread House on a Budget	*					*	*	*	*	*
Be Mine! Multiplication	*	*				*	*	*	*	*
Multiplication Menageries	*	*				*	*	*	*	*
Fall Factor Trees	*	*				*	*	*	*	*
Teeny-Tiny Times Table Books	*					*	*	*	*	*
Division Caterpillars	*					*	*	*	*	*
High Flyin' Fractions	*		*			*	*	*	*	*
Stovepipe Fraction Hats	*		*	*		*	*	*	*	*
Fraction Shape Pictures	*		*			*	*	*	*	*
Fraction Flower Bouquets	*					*	*	*	*	*
Rainbow Pattern Light Catchers		*				*	*	*	*	*
No-Sew Cross-Stitch Patterns	*	*	*			*	*	*	*	*
Growing Pattern Prints	*	*	*			*	*	*	*	*
Shifting Shapes	*		*			*	*	*	*	*
Explode-a-Square Posters	*		*			*	*	*	*	*
Great Shape Mobiles			*			*	*	*	*	*
Cube It!	*		*			*	*	*	*	*
Shapely Solids	*		*			*	*	*	*	*
Awesome Origami	*		*			*	*	*	*	*
Painting With Perspective			*	*		*	*	*	*	*
Connect-the-Dot Graph Art	*		*			*	*	*	*	*
Symmetry Circus			*			*	*	*	*	*
Paper Shape Transformations			*			*	*	*	*	*
Tessellation Ties		*	*			*	*	*	*	*
Rainbow Bead Rulers	*			*		*	*	*	*	*
Snaky Tape Measures	*			*		*	*	*	*	*
Metric Strip Sculptures	*		*	*		*	*	*	*	*
Perfect Pocket Pouches	*			*		*	*	*	*	*
Angle Art			*	*		*	*	*	*	*
Area and Perimeter Pals	*		*	*		*	*	*	*	*
Ghoulish Gloves	*			*		*	*	*	*	*
Starry Constellation Clocks				*		*	*	*	*	*
Cupcake Combinations	*	*			*	*	*	*	*	*
Leafy Venn Collages					*	*	*	*	*	*
Sand Castle Glyphs	*	*	*		*	*	*	*	*	*

100-Quill Critters

What does 100 look like? Students find out when they make these prickly pasta porcupines!

Materials

* porcupine play dough (recipe below)
* uncooked whole-wheat spaghetti
* craft glue
* craft materials (wiggle eyes, small pompoms)

1. Prepare the play dough ahead of time. Or give students measurement practice by enlisting their help.

2. Divide the class into groups. Give each group a lump of play dough about the size of a tennis ball and a supply of uncooked spaghetti. Have students shape their play dough into a porcupine body.

3. Tell them that their job is to give their porcupine 100 quills. Demonstrate how to break the spaghetti into two- to three-inch lengths and stick these "quills" into the "porcupine." Encourage each group to come up with an efficient way to reach this number (for example, *break 10 whole spaghetti strands into smaller groups of 10, count out 10 groups of 10 quills each, skip count*).

4. Let the porcupines dry completely. (This may take a day or so.) Students can then glue on wiggle eyes and pompon noses.

Teaching Tips

* Instead of using play dough, substitute one half of a 3-inch Styrofoam egg or ball for each porcupine body.

* You can use toothpicks instead of spaghetti.

Porcupine Play Dough

Makes 16 porcupines

* 8 cups flour
* 3 cups salt
* 3 cups water
* 1–2 tablespoons brown powdered tempera (optional)

Combine the flour, salt, and powdered tempera (if using) in a bowl. Add water slowly, stirring constantly. When fully combined, turn out onto a floured cutting board (or waxed paper) and knead until smooth. (To keep soft until using, seal in a plastic bag.)

Explore More

What does 1000 look like? Help students explore larger numbers by using colored spaghetti. Have students create a key to the colors and their values. For example, green = 5, orange = 10, yellow = 20.

Picture-a-Number Posters

Students create posters to help them visualize place value in different numbers.

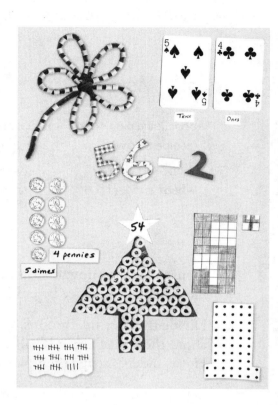

Materials

- counters or other manipulatives
- large sheets of construction paper or bulletin board paper
- craft glue and glue sticks
- crayons, colored pencils, or markers
- "number making" materials (1-cm grid paper—page 61, pipe cleaners, toothpicks, old playing cards, reproducible coins, uncooked pasta, cereal, magazines and catalogs)

1. Begin by writing a 2-digit number on the board, for example, 54. Ask students to identify the place value for each digit (*5 in the tens place, 4 in the ones place*), then write it underneath each digit and review what each represents.

2. Brainstorm other ways to represent this number. For example, five tens and four ones, 56 − 2 or 51 + 3, 54 counters or drawn dots, tally marks.

3. Tell students that they are going to design posters that represent numbers in different ways. Divide the class into groups and encourage them to use a variety of "number-making" materials to represent a specific number. (You might assign numbers to different groups according to students' ability levels, for example, 2-digit versus 3-digit numbers.)

4. Display students' posters and encourage them to compare and contrast how different numbers were represented.

Teaching Tip

Do this activity over several days, introducing it on the first day, and then inviting students to bring in items from home that they might use for their posters.

Place Value Speedway

Students explore place value to create a racecar speedway where the largest numbers take the lead!

1. Begin by writing a number on the board (as large as the place value you want to teach), for example, 513,796. Ask students to identify the place value for each digit (for example, *there is a 5 in the hundred-thousands place*). Write it underneath each digit and review what each represents.

2. Ask students how they might rearrange the digits in the example to form the largest possible number (*976,531*).

3. Tell students that they are going to create racecars that will compete on a speedway. The cars that will take the lead are those that have the largest numbers on them.

4. Divide the class into groups and give each a spinner and coloring tools. Also give each student an index card. Invite students to design and draw a racecar on their card, leaving room to write a number on the car. Students can cut out their cars, if desired.

Materials

* spinner pattern, page 10
* pencils
* brass fasteners
* 4- by 6-inch unlined index cards
* scissors
* crayons or markers
* bulletin board paper
* tape

5. Students take turns spinning the spinner and recording each digit on scrap paper. After all the spins are completed, students use their digits to make numbers with the largest value possible and write them on their cars.

6. Have group members sequence their racecars from largest number to smallest. Then have each group join with another group, combine their cars, and put them in order. Continue this process until all of the cars have been sequenced. Have group members check one another's work.

7. Enlist volunteers to design and draw a curving racetrack across the length of a sheet of bulletin board paper with a finish line at the far right. Then have students tape the cars on the speedway in order, from lowest to highest numbers, starting at the left end of the racetrack.

Teaching Tip

Depending on the place values you want students to work with, have them spin six times for numbers to the 100,000's place, five times for numbers to the 10,000's place, and so on.

Assemble the spinner using a paper clip and brass fastener as shown. Make sure the paper clip spins easily.

Gingerbread House on a Budget

Students practice money skills to "buy" ingredients for decorating their own mini "gingerbread" houses.

Materials

- Gingerbread House Price Planner, page 13
- graham crackers
- sharp knife (adult use only)
- paper plates
- plastic knives
- whipped cream cheese
- edible decorating materials in plastic bags or bowls (dried cranberries, raisins, O- and square-shaped cereal, popcorn, pretzel sticks)

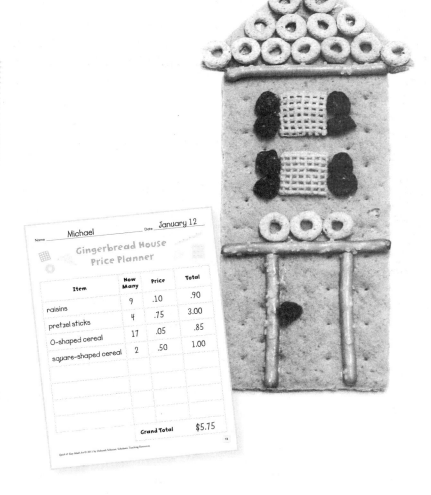

Name _____ Michael _____ Date _____ January 12 _____

Gingerbread House Price Planner

Item	How Many	Price	Total
raisins	9	.10	.90
pretzel sticks	4	.75	3.00
O-shaped cereal	17	.05	.85
square-shaped cereal	2	.50	1.00
		Grand Total	$5.75

Quick & Easy Math Art © 2011 by Deborah Schecter, Scholastic Teaching Resources

13

1. Before photocopying a class set of the budget planner, make a master for yourself and fill in the food items you will be using. Also designate a purchase price for each item that you want students to work with.

2. To make triangle "roofs," break graham crackers in half and use a sharp knife to gently saw each square in half on the diagonal. Prepare a class supply. Stock a center with whole graham crackers, triangle roofs, paper plates, plastic knives, cream cheese (to use as glue), and the decorating materials.

Teaching Tip

Check for possible food allergies before doing this activity. Or substitute paper house cutouts and craft materials for the edible items.

* Depending on the ability levels of your group, students might simply add up the purchase price of each item or multiply to arrive at their totals.

* Encourage students to sketch a picture of how they're going to decorate their house. This will help them better estimate the items they choose to use and, if they have a budget, how far their money will go.

* If desired, provide play money for students to use in making their calculations.

* Before eating their houses, students might take a digital photo to display with their planners.

3. Show students the decorating materials and tell them that they will "purchase" items to decorate a "gingerbread" house. Give each student a copy of the price planner and review the items and prices. If you want students to work within a certain budget, tell them the maximum amount they can "spend."

4. Let students visit the center in pairs. Tell them that to make their house, they need one whole graham cracker and one triangle. Then let them decide which other items, and how many, they wish to use. Have them calculate and record the total cost of each item as well as the grand total. Before they begin to decorate their houses, students should exchange planners and check each other's calculations.

5. If you set a maximum budget, discuss the decorating choices students made. Did price affect their buying decisions?

Explore More

Challenge students to figure out the total cost of all the gingerbread houses the class made.

Name _____ Date _____

Gingerbread House
Price Planner

Item	How Many	Price	Total
	Grand Total		

Be Mine! Multiplication

Students use arrays to create heart-filled valentines that help them conceptualize multiplication facts.

Materials

* heart pattern, page 15 (copied onto pink or red cardstock, or glued to cardboard)

* small candy conversation hearts (or small heart stickers)

* craft glue or glue dots

* crayons, colored pencils, or markers

1. Explain that an array is an arrangement of objects in rows and columns that can be used to show a multiplication fact. Draw a few examples on the board and ask students to tell the multiplication fact each represents.

4 x 6   6 x 4

2. Give each student a heart pattern and a supply of candy hearts or heart stickers. Invite students to choose a multiplication fact to represent (or assign one to each student).

3. Have students arrange the hearts in arrays to represent their fact and glue them in place. Then they write the multiplication problem on the lines provided, decorate their heart, and write the name of the person to whom they wish to give their valentine.

Explore More

Have students make valentine-rhyme flash cards. Invite them to come up with their own valentine verses that rhyme with specific multiplication products, then use candy hearts, stickers, or drawings to illustrate and write equations for them on paper heart cutouts.

Roses are red
I think you're great!
8 x 6 = 48

Roses are red
Violets are blue.
9 x 8 = 72

Roses are red
Clovers are green
3 x 6 = 18

Teaching Tip

Using candy conversation hearts, the heart pattern will accommodate arrays for products up to 32. For higher numbers, enlarge the pattern or have students use markers to draw smaller hearts or X's and O's. Having students use markers to draw their own hearts is also a good option if you to want students to practice a variety of facts.

Heart pattern

To: _____

From: _____

How many times
Do I wish you'd be mine?

_____ × _____ = _____

Will you be my Valentine?

Multiplication Menageries

Math, art, and science combine when students create models of creepy crawly bugs and other critters to explore multiplication using equal sets.

Materials

- pictures or photographs of different bugs and animals
- scissors
- craft glue
- craft materials (quick-drying modeling clay, construction paper, tissue paper, pipe cleaners, toothpicks, glitter glue, yarn, crayons or markers)

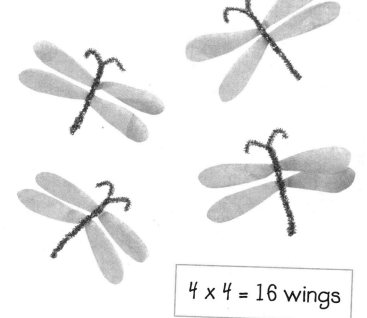

4 x 4 = 16 wings

1. Share with students images of different kinds of bugs and animals and discuss their attributes. For example, dragonflies have two pairs of wings for a total of four; ants and beetles have six legs; starfish have five arms; spiders have eight legs; inchworms have 10 legs.

2. Demonstrate that multiplication is actually repeated addition by drawing a simple picture of two spiders on the board. Ask students how many legs the spiders have in all. (*8 + 8 = 16*) Draw a third spider and repeat the process. (*8 + 8 + 8 = 24*) Then ask students to give a multiplication fact that describes each picture. (*2 x 8; 3 x 8*)

Teaching Tip

Point out that the numbers multiplied in each multiplication fact are called *factors*. In these examples, the first factor represents the number of sets and the second factor represents the number of items in the set.

3. Provide students with craft materials and invite them to create different bugs or other animals (real or imaginary) that can be used to represent multiplication facts (or assign facts to students). They can create two-dimensional projects and glue to a paper background or three-dimensional models to place on a tray. Examples of bugs and animals and their attributes students might create:

Snail: 2 antennae

Bee: Students might make bees that each have 3 stripes.

Dragonfly: 4 wings

Starfish: 5 arms

Ant: 6 legs

Caterpillar: Students might design imaginary caterpillars that each have 7 body sections.

Spider or Octopus: 8 legs

Ladybug: Students might draw ladybugs that have 9 dots each.

Crab or Inchworm: 10 legs

$3 \times 8 = 24$ legs

4. Have students write the multiplication fact that describes their critter creations on their paper or on a card to accompany the project. Invite students to share their creations with the class and explain how their critters represent the multiplication fact they chose.

$5 \times 2 = 10$ antennae

Explore More

Extend the activity to relate skip counting to multiplication by asking students to count, for example, their snails by 2's or their starfish by 5's.

Fall Factor Trees

Students create colorful fall trees to explore factors and prime numbers.

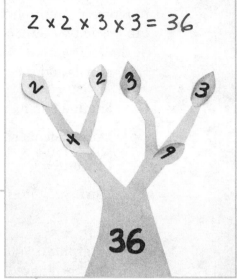

$$2 \times 2 \times 3 \times 3 = 36$$

Materials

* construction paper (assorted fall colors including yellow, red, orange, and brown)
* scissors
* markers
* glue sticks

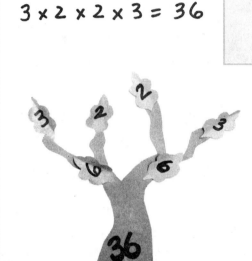

$$3 \times 2 \times 2 \times 3 = 36$$

1. Begin by introducing or reviewing factors and prime numbers:

   * Factors are numbers that you multiply together to equal another number. For example, 1 x 8 = 8 and 2 x 4 = 8. The numbers 1, 2, 4, and 8 are all factors of 8. Point out to students that a factor divides evenly into another number: 1, 2, 4, and 8 all divide evenly into 8.

   * A prime number is any number greater than 1 that has only two factors—itself and 1. For example, 1 x 5 = 5. No other whole numbers divide evenly into 5.

Teaching Tip

This activity lays the foundation for a deeper understanding of prime and composite numbers that students will study later on in school.

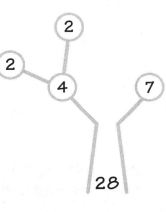

2. Model for students how to create a factor tree for the number 28 using the factors 4 and 7. Draw a simple diagram on the board, as shown. Guide them to understand how to complete each branch. What do students notice once they reach 2 and 7? (*No more branches can be added because these are both prime numbers.*) Then point out that when each of the prime numbers on the tree are multiplied by one another (2 x 2 x 7) they equal the product, 28.

3. Repeat step 2 using a different set of factors for 28, for example, 2 and 14. Guide students to notice that the final branches contain the same prime numbers.

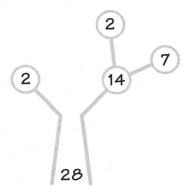

4. Tell students that they will explore factors by making their own fall factor trees. Have each student choose a different multiplication product (or assign products to students). Tell students to sketch a factor tree diagram for their product on scrap paper using the example from step 2 as a model.

5. Let them choose a sheet of construction paper to use as a background and then draw and cut out a tree trunk and fall leaves from other paper in colors of their choice (one leaf for each factor to go on their tree). Tell them to use their sketch as a guide to how big the trunk and leaves can be.

6. Using their diagram as a guide, have students write their product on the tree trunk, draw branches, and glue on leaves that have been labeled with the factors. Have them continue drawing branches and adding factor leaves until they have only prime numbers.

7. At the top of their paper, have students write a multiplication expression that shows how the product of the prime numbers on their factor tree equals their product. If some students made factor trees for the same product, have them compare and contrast the appearance of their trees. Guide them to notice that the final factors (prime numbers) are always the same.

Teaching Tips

❋ To add dimension to the leaves, students can fold them in half the long way, use a fingernail to make a crease, and then reopen.

❋ Instead of drawing the branches, students might want to include them when they draw and cut out their trees from paper.

Teeny-Tiny Times Table Books

Students will love practicing multiplication facts with these miniature times table books that they can wear around their necks!

Materials

* book cover pattern, page 21, copied onto heavyweight paper or cardstock
* 3- by 3-inch self-stick note pads
* scissors
* straightedge
* hot-glue gun (adult use only)
* small, self-adhesive Velcro dots
* 36-inch lengths of yarn

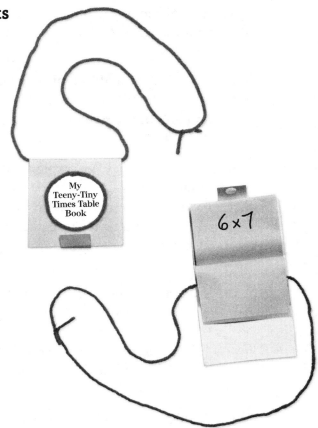

Model for students how to make the books:

1. Fold inward along the solid lines and use a straightedge to make sharp creases.

2. Apply hot glue (adult use only) inside the spine of the book cover. Then center the yarn along the spine and press it into the glue.

3. Apply hot glue to the spine and the back cover of the note pad, leaving the front cover and tab unglued. Then place the note pad's spine on top of the yarn on the book cover spine.

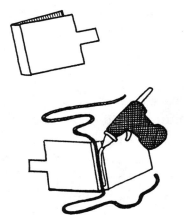

4. Wrap the book cover around the note pad. Let the glue cool and harden completely.

5. Title the book, "My Teeny-Tiny Times Table Book."

6. To keep the book closed, attach small self-adhesive Velcro dots to the tab and the book cover.

7. Tie the ends of the yarn to make a necklace that fits loosely around your neck. To record multiplication facts you need to practice, position the book so the spine faces you. Then use a pencil to write a fact on each page and the answer on the back.

Encourage students to wear their book necklaces and open them often to review their times table facts.

Teaching Tip

When students write their facts, have them bend back each page up to the sticky area (not all the way to the spine of the book). This will ensure that pages do not slip out. (See photo on opposite page.)

Explore More

Have students add division facts they need to practice to their books.

Book Cover pattern

Division Caterpillars

These handy critters hold division facts students need to practice and then fold up to tuck in a pocket when not in use.

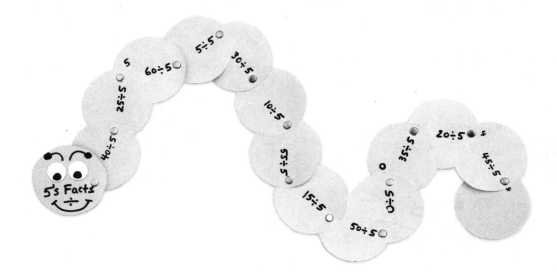

 Materials

For each caterpillar:

* unlined index cards or cardstock, assorted colors

* 3-inch circle template (jar lids work well)

* 14 small brass fasteners

* hole punch

* markers

Show students how to make their caterpillars:

1. For a division fact family covering facts with divisors from 0–12, trace and cut out 15 circles from index cards or cardstock.

2. Make the caterpillar's head. Choose a division fact family you want to practice and write it on the first circle. Draw eyes and antennae, then punch a hole on the right side of the head, close to the edge.

3. Punch two holes opposite each other and near the edge of 13 of the circles. Punch one hole in the remaining circle.

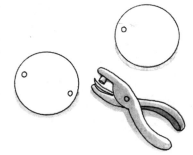

4. Write the division facts for the fact family in order from 0–12 on each of 13 circles. The 14th circle will be blank.

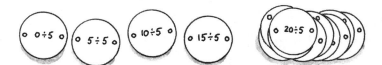

5. Scramble the fact card circles. Then use the brass fasteners to connect all of the circles, overlapping them left over right.

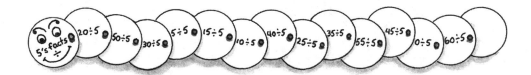

6. Write the answer to each fact on the next circle to the right, so it's hidden in the section where the circles overlap. On the 14th circle, write the answer to the last fact.

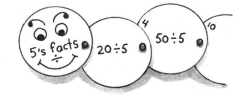

7. To use the caterpillar, fold it up so that all of the sections are stacked under the head. Then, starting at the head, slide open one section at a time, practice the fact, and then slide open the next section to check the answer. Next, practice the fact on that section, check the answer on the next section, and so on, until the caterpillar is fully extended.

Explore More

Invite students to make fold-up caterpillars to practice multiplication facts.

High Flyin' Fractions

Students design kites and hot air balloons that will help them develop an understanding of equivalent fractions.

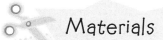

Materials

* 8-inch squares and circles of copy paper
* crayons or markers
* construction paper
* scissors
* tape
* yarn or string
* glue

1. Fold a square of paper in half, unfold, and draw a line on the fold. Ask students how many equal parts they see. (*2*) Point out that each part is $\frac{1}{2}$. Repeat the process with a paper circle.

2. Refold each shape and fold in half again. Then unfold and draw another line. How many equal parts are there now? (*4; each section represents $\frac{1}{4}$*) Ask students to predict how many equal parts there will be if you refold the shapes once more. (*8; each section is $\frac{1}{8}$*)

3. Give students paper squares and circles and let them experiment folding the shapes a different number of times and in different ways to create equal fractional parts.

4. Invite students to design kites and/or hot air balloons with their shapes. Have them repeat step 3, but this time create a pattern on the squares and circles by coloring the sections formed by folding the shapes.

5. Have students add yarn (or string) tails and construction paper bows to their kites, and yarn ropes and construction paper baskets to their hot air balloons, affixing them using glue or tape. Also have them label their project with the fractional parts represented.

6. Create a "High Flyin' Fractions" display to showcase students' work. Ask students to share how many equal parts their designs have and to use a fraction to describe one part.

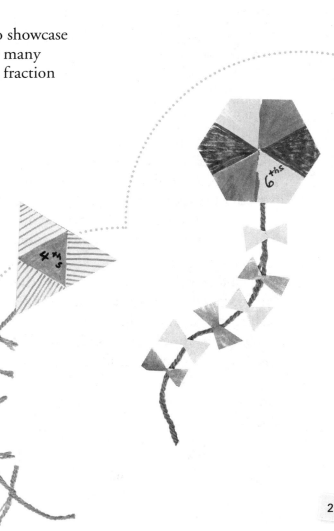

Explore More

Let students explore making kites and hot air balloons using ovals, hexagons, and other shapes.

Stovepipe Fraction Hats

Hats off! These colorful hats let students use their hands to recognize that fractions can represent parts of a whole.

Materials

- *The Cat in the Hat* by Dr. Seuss
- 9- by 12-inch white construction paper
- 9- by 12-inch pieces of tagboard
- 2- by 12-inch white construction paper strips (for the hat brim)
- blank sentence strips (for the headband)
- rulers
- sets of red paper strips (or any color other than white) See Teaching Tip, below.
- scissors
- craft glue and glue sticks
- strong tape

1. Show students the stovepipe hat in *The Cat in the Hat*. Ask: "What fraction is represented by the pattern of stripes on the hat?" (*fifths*) Tell students that they are going to make their own "Cat in the Hat" hats to represent different fractions.

2. Draw a few rectangles, positioned vertically, on the board. Ask students to describe ways to divide each rectangle into striped fractional parts similar to the hat in the Seuss book. Invite volunteers to come up and show their ideas.

Teaching Tip

Ahead of time prepare sets of red paper strips. For example:

- For a "halves" hat: one 6- by 9-inch strip
- For a "3rds" hat: two 4- by 9-inch strips
- For a "4ths" hat: two 3- by 9-inch strips
- For a "6ths" hat: three 2- by 9-inch strips
- For an "8ths" hat: four $1\frac{1}{2}$- by 9-inch strips
- For a "12ths" hat: six 1- by 9-inch strips

Or, give students measurement practice by enlisting their help.

halves   3rds   4ths   5ths   6ths

3. Give each student a sheet of white construction paper, a piece of tagboard, a white "brim" strip, a sentence strip, and a ruler. Then have students choose a set of red paper strips. (Or assign specific fractions to students.) Also provide scissors, craft glue, glue sticks, and tape. Have students follow these instructions:

Teaching Tip

Have students measure the height of their strips (1 inch, $1\frac{1}{2}$ inches, 2 inches, and so on). Guide them to understand that the height of the spaces between the strips needs to be the same.

- Glue the white paper to the tagboard. This will be the striped part of your hat.

- What fraction will your hat show? Use a ruler to space the colored strips evenly on the hat. Then glue them down.

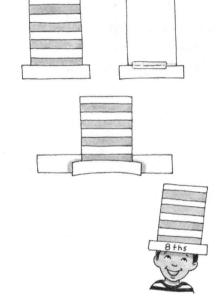

- Center the striped hat above the brim, then tape together on the back.

- Center the assembled hat on the sentence strip and line up the bottom edges of both pieces. Then glue the hat to the sentence strip, leaving $1\frac{1}{2}$ inches free on each end of the brim.

- Write on the brim the fractional parts displayed on your hat. Then ask a friend to help you overlap and tape the sentence strip closed around your head.

4. Have a hat show! Invite students to don their hats. Discuss the different fractions represented and how the height of the stripes corresponds to the fractions shown.

Explore More

Challenge students to explore other ways to divide the stovepipe shape into fractional parts.

Have students use rulers and pencils to divide the white rectangle into the fraction of their choosing, then color the sections as desired.

Fraction Shape Pictures

Students snip paper to create pictures and equations using fractional parts.

Materials

* 6-inch construction paper squares, circles, hexagons, and triangles and 6- by 8-inch rectangles in assorted colors
* construction paper (for a background)
* rulers
* scissors
* pencils
* crayons, colored pencils, or markers
* glue sticks

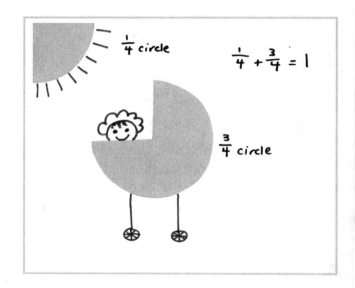

1. Draw a few squares, rectangles, and circles on the board. Ask students to tell how each shape might be divided in half and in fourths. Invite volunteers to come up and show their ideas.

2. Tell students that they will divide construction shapes into fractional parts, cut them apart, and then use their imagination to create a picture with the pieces. They will use all of the pieces to equal one whole and then write an equation that describes their picture.

3. Have each student choose a shape. Encourage students to consider the best ways to cut their shapes into equal-sized fractional parts. For example, they might fold the paper in half or quarters and then cut out the pieces. Or they might use a ruler and pencil to divide the shape into fractional sections, then cut it apart.

4. Tell students to arrange their shapes in different ways on their background paper. This process is bound to spark ideas. When they come up with a picture they like, have them glue the shapes to the paper and add details using crayons or markers.

5. Have students label each part of their pictures with the fractional part of the whole it represents and then write a math equation that describes it.

Teaching Tip

Instead of construction paper, students might use patterned gift wrap or origami paper to make their pictures.

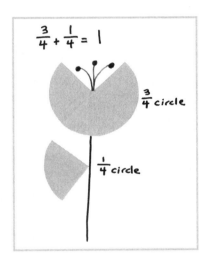

$$\frac{3}{4} + \frac{1}{4} = 1$$

$\frac{3}{4}$ circle

$\frac{1}{4}$ circle

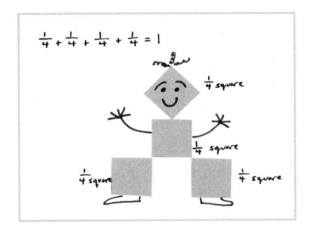

$$\frac{1}{4} + \frac{1}{4} + \frac{1}{4} + \frac{1}{4} = 1$$

$\frac{1}{4}$ square

$\frac{1}{4}$ square

$\frac{1}{4}$ square

$\frac{1}{4}$ square

$$\frac{1}{8} + \frac{1}{8} + \frac{1}{8} + \frac{1}{8} + \frac{1}{8} + \frac{1}{8} + \frac{1}{8} + \frac{1}{8} = 1$$

8 eighths of a square

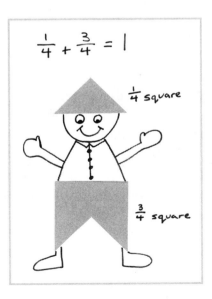

$$\frac{1}{4} + \frac{3}{4} = 1$$

$\frac{1}{4}$ square

$\frac{3}{4}$ square

Fraction Flower Bouquets

Students design beautiful blooms as they develop an understanding of fractions as parts of a group.

Materials

- 3-inch construction paper squares in assorted colors
- scissors
- crayons, colored pencils, or markers
- green pipe cleaners
- empty 20 oz. plastic water or soda bottles (labels removed)

1. Review the concepts of numerators and denominators. On chart paper or the whiteboard, draw a simple picture of a group of flowers. Color some of the flowers differently to reflect fractional parts of the group. See examples at right.

2. Ask students what fraction of the flowers is yellow ($\frac{3}{5}$) and what fraction is pink ($\frac{2}{5}$). Model how to write these fractions. Remind students that when a fraction represents a part of a group, the denominator (bottom number) tells the total number in the group, and the numerator (top number) tells how many are in a set that's part of the group—in this case, flowers of a particular color.

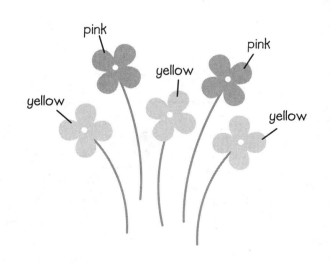

3. Tell students that they are going to create a multi-colored bouquet of flowers that represents different fractions. Have students choose two or three different colors of paper squares. Then have them make flowers by following these steps:

- Fold a paper square in half, then in half again.

- Draw the shape of a petal on the folded paper. The shape should start on one of the folded edges and end on the other folded edge. Be sure not to draw all the way to the folded corner.

- Cut out the shape, through all of the layers, and unfold the resulting flower. Decorate, if desired.

- Punch a hole through the center of the flower.

- Poke a pipe cleaner through the hole and curl or bend the end to hold the flower on the stem.

4. When students have completed their bouquet, have them insert the stems in a plastic bottle, then add a construction paper label that describes, in fractions, the color of the flowers in their bouquet.

Teaching Tips

❋ Depending on students' abilities, you might tell them to make a specific number of flowers and how many of each color.

❋ As an added challenge, ask students to reduce fractions to their lowest terms.

Explore More

As a variation, have students each make five or six flowers in one color of their choice. Then they can team up with one or more other students and put their flowers together in different combinations. Have them determine what fractional part of their combined bouquets is a specific color. Encourage them to change the number of flowers and colors in their group bouquet several times to come up with different fractional parts.

Rainbow Pattern Light Catchers

Students experiment with repeated patterns as they mix colors to create the colors of the rainbow.

Materials

* red, yellow, and blue transparent plastic sheets (report covers work well), cut into 1- by 6-inch strips, 4 strips of each color per student
* white construction paper
* scissors
* tape
* construction paper

1. Ask students if they have ever seen a rainbow. If so, where did they see it, and what did they see? Show students photographs or pictures of rainbows and help them identify the colors—red, orange, yellow, green, blue, and violet.

2. Hand out a red, yellow, and blue plastic strip to each student. Challenge students to create rainbow colors by overlapping the strips in different ways. What colors do they see? (*Overlapping yellow and blue make green; red and yellow make orange; blue and red make violet.*)

3. Give each student a sheet of white construction paper. Then distribute 9 more strips (3 each of red, yellow, blue) so that students have 12 strips in all. Show them how to arrange the strips in a color pattern that can be used to create a rainbow-like checkerboard design.

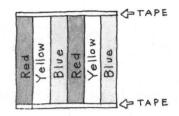

- On the white paper, lay 6 strips side by side vertically, alternating red, yellow, and blue strips to create a square.

- Carefully tape the ends of the strips together.

- Lay 6 more strips horizontally on top of the first set of strips. Begin with red and alternate the colors following the same pattern as before to create a checkerboard design.

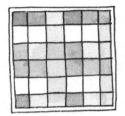

- Tape the ends together to hold the strips in place.

4. Ask students to describe the pattern of colors they created in each row. Encourage them to notice how the colors alternate and then repeat every three rows.

5. Have students choose a sheet of construction paper in the color of their choice and cut out a shape, such as a fish, heart, or star. Then show them how to fold the paper in half, cut out a half circle or abstract shape from the middle, and unfold.

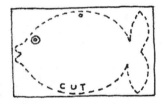
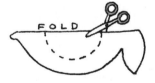

6. Tell students to tape the rainbow pattern to the back of the paper shape so that the colors show through the opening, then cut off any excess. Tape the designs to a window and watch them catch the light!

Explore More

Invite students to make more complex patterns using the colored strips. They can cut strips in different widths and experiment overlapping them in different ways to create different effects.

No-Sew Cross-Stitch Patterns

**The age-old craft of cross-stitch is perfect
for an exploration of repeated patterns.**

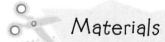 Materials

* $\frac{1}{4}$ -inch grid paper, page 36
* colored pencils or markers

Optional:

* cardstock or tagboard
* scissors
* glue sticks
* construction paper

1. If possible, show students photographs of cross-stitch samplers
    with borders that have repeating patterns as well as Native
    American beaded designs. Encourage students to describe the
    patterns they see and notice how they repeat. Then tell them
    that they are going to create cross-stitch patterns on paper.

Teaching Tip

Instead of using X's,
students might color in the
boxes on the grid paper to
create their designs.

2. Copy a sheet of grid paper onto
    transparency film or scan for use on a
    whiteboard. Demonstrate how to make
    a simple pattern by drawing colored X's
    in the squares on the grid. Point out
    how both color and shape can be used
    to make a design that repeats. Start a
    few patterns and invite volunteers to
    continue them.

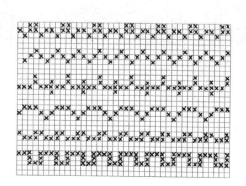

3. Provide students with sheets of grid paper and colored pencils or markers and invite them to create repeating cross-stitch designs of their own. Students can then turn their designs into a variety of decorative items:

Teaching Tip

Have students sketch their patterns in pencil before using coloring tools.

- **Sampler:** Create a repeating border around the edges of a sheet of grid paper. Inside the border, experiment using cross-stitch to create designs, pictures, and letters to write a name or greeting. Mount on construction paper.

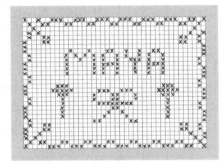

- **Bracelet or Armband:** Make a repeating design about 5 to 6 squares tall along the short edge of the grid paper. Cut out the section of the grid with your pattern and glue it to a strip of same-sized cardstock or tagboard. Attach the strip to your wrist or arm with a piece of tape.

- **Belt:** Repeat the directions above but make several same-sized patterns along the length of the grid paper. Cut out and glue the patterned strips end to end to make one long strip and then glue to a strip of cardstock or tagboard. Trim to fit around your waist and punch a hole in each end. Use brass fasteners to fasten the belt.

- **Cross-Stitch Pictures:** Celebrate different holidays by drawing a large outline of a stocking, holiday tree, gift, heart, or egg. Fill the shape with repeating rows of cross-stitch patterns, then cut out the shape.

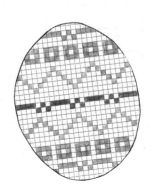
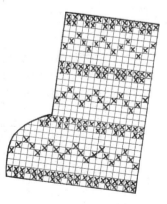

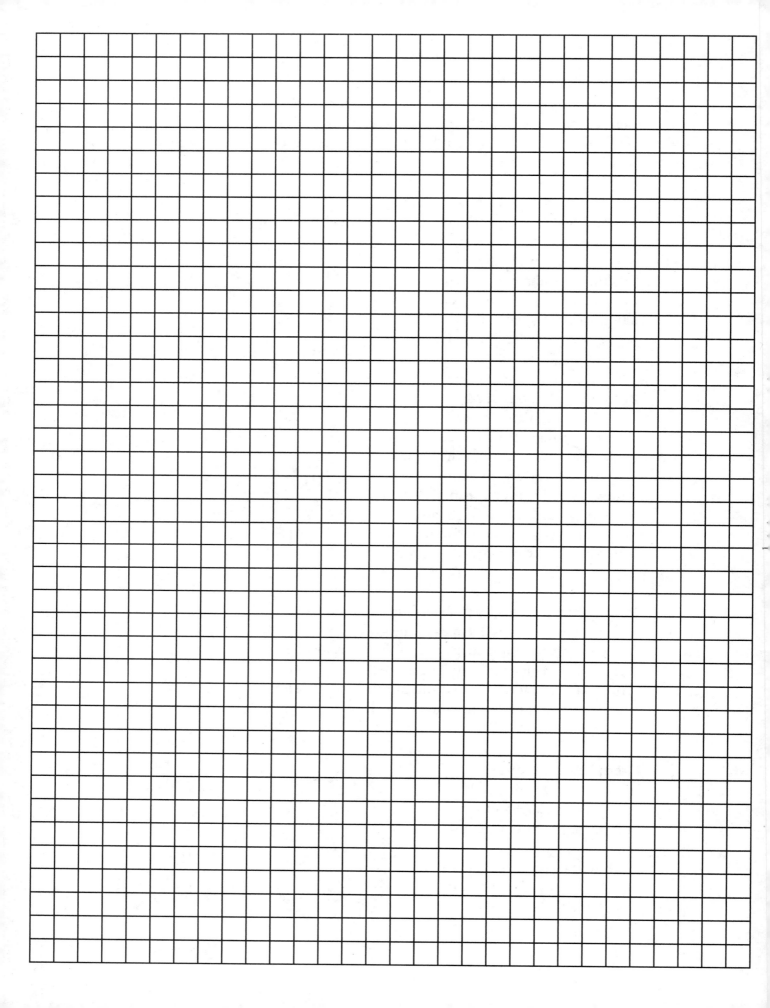

Growing Pattern Prints

Students explore growing patterns as they make printed designs.

✂️ ## Materials

- ❋ pattern-making materials and tools (shape stamps, stickers, craft paper punches, construction paper scraps)
- ❋ crayons, colored pencils, or markers
- ❋ scissors
- ❋ glue sticks
- ❋ large sheets of construction or bulletin board paper (for a background)

Dino Age	Number of Spikes
1	3
2	4
3	5
4	6
5	7

My dinosaur had 3 spikes when it was 1 year old. It grows 1 spike each year. To get the number of spikes, you add 2 to its age. At age 6, it would have 8 spikes.

1. Begin by modeling a few examples of growing patterns using pattern blocks, interlocking cubes, or by drawing simple shapes on the board. (See samples, below.) Invite volunteers to describe and continue each pattern. Ask students to articulate a rule for how each pattern grows.

2. Show students how to make a table for each pattern that will help them see the numerical relationships in a growing pattern. Point out how the growing numbers on the table correspond to the growing picture patterns.

Teaching Tip

Using a table sets the stage for working with functions. Depending on your students' skill level with growing patterns, you may or may not want to introduce them to the table.

Pattern	Number of Circles
1	4
2	5
3	6
4	7

Pattern	Number of Squares
1	3
2	6
3	10
4	15

Pattern	Number of Shapes
1	3
2	5
3	7
4	9

3. Tell students to think of a pattern (either a design or picture) they would like to make and how they might make it grow. Have them use manipulatives, such as pattern blocks or counters to map it out. Or they can sketch their pattern on paper. Encourage them to make a table to record information about their patterns and/or describe their pattern rule in writing.

4. Provide students with materials and tools for making patterns. Students might print their patterns using shape stamps, or use stickers or paper shapes (cut using craft punches or scissors), or simply draw them. Encourage students to grow their pattern at least four or five times.

5. Display students' patterns and companion tables on a "How Do Our Patterns Grow?" bulletin board. Discuss each pattern with students. Which parts of the pattern remain the same? Which parts grow? Challenge students to identify and explain the pattern rule and predict what would come next to keep it growing.

Teaching Tip

You might provide students with a few examples of both simple and more complex growing patterns for them to replicate and then extend.

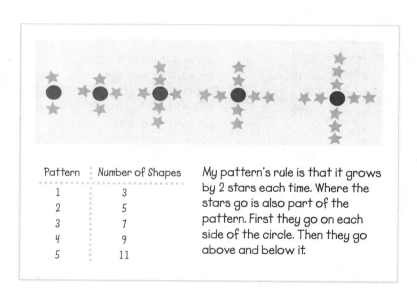

Pattern	Number of Shapes
1	3
2	5
3	7
4	9
5	11

My pattern's rule is that it grows by 2 stars each time. Where the stars go is also part of the pattern. First they go on each side of the circle. Then they go above and below it.

Day	Number of Snowflakes
1	2
2	5
3	10
4	17
5	26
6	37

My pattern starts with 2 snowflakes. The rule is that it grows by 3 snowflakes, then 5, then 7, then 9, then 11.

My pattern starts with 1 leaf in a pot made of 2 squares. The rule is that it alternates growing each day by 2 leaves and then by 1 leaf.

Day	Number of Shapes
1	3
2	5
3	6
4	8
5	9
6	11

Shifting Shapes

**Students overlap transparent shapes to see
how many different new shapes they can create.**

Materials

❋ red, yellow, and blue
  colored transparent
  shapes (report covers
  work well), cut into
  triangles, circles,
  rectangles, and squares
  in different sizes

1. Give each student two colored, transparent
   squares to overlap as shown at right. What shape
   do students see in the overlapping portion? (*a
   rectangle*) Then ask them to move the squares in
   different ways to see how many different kinds
   of rectangles they can make. Samples of possible
   arrangements are shown below.

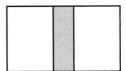

2. What other shapes can students make by overlapping the squares in different ways? Examples include a square, different kinds of triangles, kite (diamond), pentagon, and hexagon. (You might use an overhead projector to let students share their discoveries with the class.) Which shapes were easiest to create? More difficult?

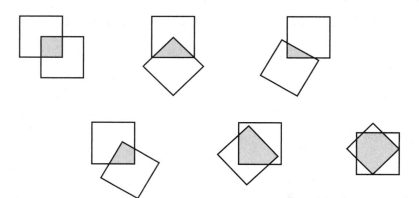

Teaching Tip

You might have students take a digital photo to make a visual record of their shape designs, then make a slide show to present their findings to the class.

3. Repeat steps 1 and 2 using rectangles, and then different types of triangles. Pose challenges, such as "Can you overlap two triangles to make a square? A parallelogram?"

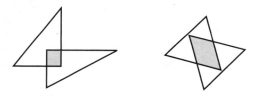

4. Let students explore using two or more different sizes of each shape, and then using different shapes, such as a square and a circle, to see how that affects the kinds of shapes they can make. Have students draw pictures to keep track of the different shapes they come up with.

5. You can create temporary window displays of students' designs while teaching two quick science lessons!

- On a dry day, have students rub the plastic shapes on their hair or a wool sweater, then press them onto the glass. Static electricity charges will make the shapes hold on tight!

- To demonstrate adhesion at work, wet the back of the plastic shapes and press them to the glass. They will stick until the water evaporates.

Explode-a-Square Posters

Students deconstruct squares by cutting them apart and rearranging them to form new designs.

 Materials

* 4-inch construction paper squares, (three for each student, plus extras; see Teaching Tip, below)
* 12- by 18-inch construction paper (for a background)
* scissors
* glue stick

1. Fold a square of paper in half, unfold it, then cut along the fold to form two rectangles. Repeat the process with another square, but fold it in half from one corner to the opposite corner, then cut it on the diagonal. Ask students to identify the resulting shapes. (*2 rectangles and 2 triangles*) Ask: "Are the two halves of the square the same?" Place one on top of the other to show that the halves are congruent—the same size and shape.

Teaching Tip

Prepare a demonstration set of paper squares, cut apart in different ways as shown:

2. Repeat step 1 with another square, this time folding and cutting it into quarters. Ask students to identify the resulting shapes. (*4 smaller squares*)

3. Invite volunteers to take turns making a design with each cut-apart square. Guide students to notice that although the resulting configuration may no longer resemble a square, nothing was added or taken away from the original square—it was just cut into smaller parts. Each design they make is composed entirely of the components of one square.

4. Show students how to fold and cut apart a paper square into other smaller, equal-sized parts. Then give them a set of three squares and a sheet of construction paper to use for a background. Invite them to experiment folding and cutting each square apart, and then moving the parts around to create unusual designs. (Explain that they should not mix the parts from different squares to make each design.)

5. When students are satisfied with the different designs they created, have them glue them to construction paper, leaving spaces between them.

6. Display the posters and compare and contrast the different configurations and effects created.

Teaching Tips

❊ Depending on the sizes and shapes of students' designs, they may need a larger or smaller sheet of background paper.

❊ Instead of squares, give students paper circles to cut apart and rearrange to form different designs.

Explore More

Explode-a-Shape Banners

Repeat the activity but have students use squares and circles in two different colors. They cut apart three or four squares or circles of the same color and mount the arrangements on a contrasting color and shape. Have students use yarn and tape to connect each shape, one below the other.

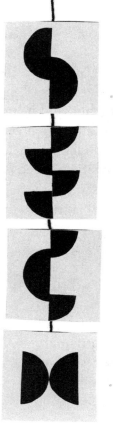

Great Shape Mobiles

Students explore topology as they snip a folded square to create a three-dimensional mobile that whirls in the wind!

Materials

❋ 8- or 9-inch heavyweight paper or cardstock squares

❋ scissors

❋ string

❋ tape

Show students a paper square and a completed mobile. Tell them that one paper square was used to make the three-dimensional shape. Ask them to think about ways this might be done and to share their ideas. Then let them try it themselves. Give each student a paper square and scissors. Also provide tape, thin yarn or string, and glue. Have students follow these steps:

Teaching Tip

For a decorative effect, before folding and cutting the paper, invite students to decorate both sides with paints, crayons, or markers. Or, use gold and silver metallic paper or paper that's a different color on each side.

1. Fold the square into quarters. (Fold it in half and then in half again.)

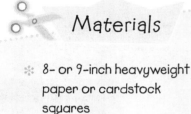

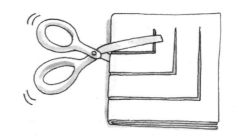

2. Starting from the doubled-folded edges, make three or more perpendicular cuts into the square, stopping about $\frac{1}{4}$ inch from the middle fold.

3. Open the folded square and flatten it.

4. Gently bend back each of the inner square frames so that they are at opposite angles to each other.

5. Tape a piece of string to your mobile, then hang it near a window and watch it whirl!

Explore More

* Invite students to make circle-, oval-, and rectangle-shaped mobiles.

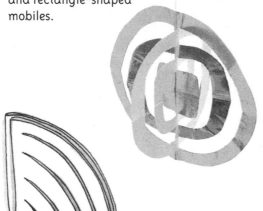

* Explore topology in another way. Fold a paper shape, such as an evergreen tree or a fish, in half, and make parallel cuts along the length of the fold. Then push every other folded flap inward, as shown.

Cube It!

Students build spatial reasoning and visualization skills as they create cube boxes using two-dimensional nets they design.

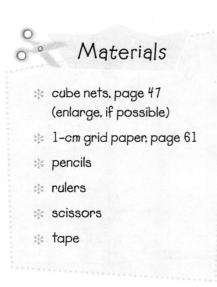

Materials

* cube nets, page 47 (enlarge, if possible)
* 1-cm grid paper, page 61
* pencils
* rulers
* scissors
* tape

1. Show students a square of paper and a cube made from folded paper. Explain that when talking about the flat surfaces of a three-dimensional figure, the term *face* is used instead of *side*, and *vertex* (*vertices*, plural) is used to describe a corner. (*Side* and *corner* are used in describing a two-dimensional figure such as a square.) The place where two faces come together is called an *edge*. Have students identify the properties of each figure and record their responses on a chart.

Teaching Tips

* Give students a copy of the 3-D Detectives Record Sheet, page 50, and have them fill in a section with information about cubes.

* Mask the numbers on the grid paper before photocopying, if desired.

Square	Cube
Flat (2-D)	Solid (3-D)
1 side	6 faces
4 edges	12 edges
4 corners	8 vertices
length, width	length, width, height

2. Give each student a copy of the net pattern page, scissors, and tape. Explain that each pattern is called a *net*. Ask, "How are the nets alike and different? Which nets do you think will fold into a cube?" Have students share and explain the reasons for their predictions, then cut out the nets and test them. (Nets A and B work, C and D do not.)

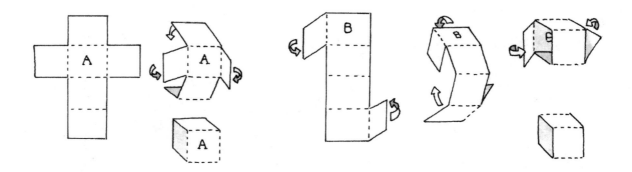

3. Divide the class into groups and provide multiple copies of the grid paper. Challenge students to use rulers and pencils to design nets that will fold into cubes, and then test them out. Encourage them to refer to the chart from step 1, as well as the nets in step 2, and apply what they learned about the properties of a cube. Also encourage them to analyze designs that do not work and think about ways to adapt them.

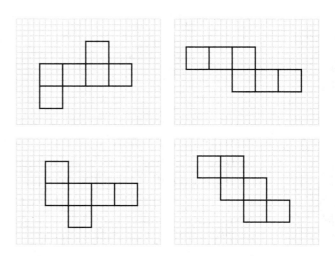

There are 11 possible net designs that will fold up to form cubes.

4. Afterward, bring the class together and have students share their discoveries. Have them sort their net designs into two groups—designs that worked and designs that didn't. Encourage students to study the successful designs and notice characteristics they share. What did they learn from the nets that did not work?

5. Let students use their imaginations to turn their successful net designs into a variety of creative projects. Enlarge and copy the nets (or glue) onto heavyweight paper. Then invite students to decorate them before assembly. See page 49 for ideas.

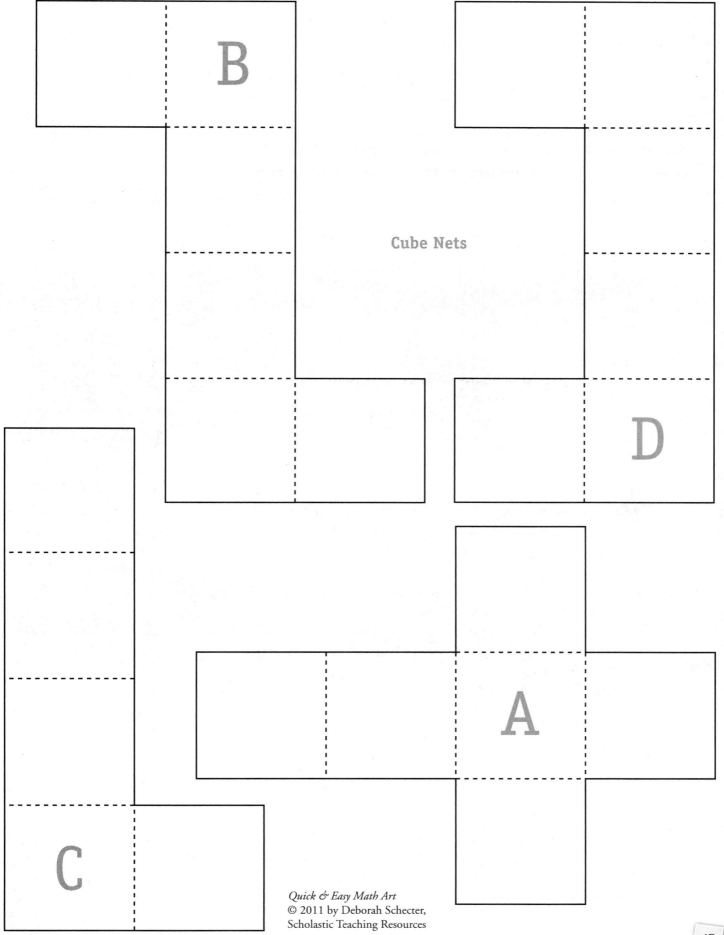

Cube Nets

Quick & Easy Math Art
© 2011 by Deborah Schecter,
Scholastic Teaching Resources

Shapely Solids

Students compare two- and three-dimensional figures as they make festive ornaments, fanciful creatures, and more.

✂ Materials

- 3-D Detectives Record Sheet, page 50
- triangular pyramid net, page 51
- triangular prism net, page 52

- scissors
- tape or glue sticks
- craft materials (shape stamps, stickers, crayons, markers, glitter glue, recycled gift wrap)

1. Give each student a copy of the net pages. Ask students to identify and count the shapes on each. Can they predict the solid figure that can be formed from each net?

2. Have students cut out each net along the solid lines, fold inward along the dotted lines, then use tape or a glue stick to affix the flaps to the inside of the figure. How did students' predictions compare with each resulting solid? Tell students the name of each figure: *triangular pyramid* (also called a *tetrahedron*) and *triangular prism.*

Teaching Tip

If possible, copy or glue the patterns onto heavyweight paper to make them more durable.

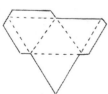

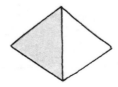
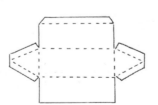
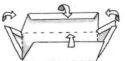
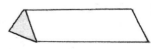

3. To help students focus on the properties of each figure, have them fill in the record sheet. (Students might use pencils to lightly mark each vertex and edge as they count to help them keep track.) Afterward, have students share the data on their record sheets. Encourage students to make other observations about each figure (types of angles, parallel lines, symmetry, and so on). Also have them observe similarities and differences between the two-dimensional figures on the nets and the three-dimensional figures they made.

4. Give students additional copies of the net patterns and invite them to transform them in decorative ways:

- **Solid Shape Sculptures:** Glue one or more nets to the back of recycled gift wrap. Fold and assemble. Then glue two or more figures together to make an ornament or sculpture.

- **Gift Boxes:** Decorate a net using shape stamps, stickers, crayons or markers, or glitter glue. Assemble, then put a small gift inside, and seal closed with a sticker, a paper sleeve, or ribbon.

- **Feathered Friends & More:** Use craft items to transform the solid figures into birds, fish, and other creatures.

Teaching Tip

Students can use the other two sections on the record sheet to fill in information about a cube (see page 45) and another solid they might investigate.

3-D Detectives Record Sheet

Record what you observe about 3-D figures.

Name of Solid Figure:

- -

number and shape
of faces

number of edges

number of vertices
(corners)

Name of Solid Figure:

- -

number and shape
of faces

number of edges

number of vertices
(corners)

Name of Solid Figure:

- -

number and shape
of faces

number of edges

number of vertices
(corners)

Name of Solid Figure:

- -

number and shape
of faces

number of edges

number of vertices
(corners)

Triangular Pyramid Net

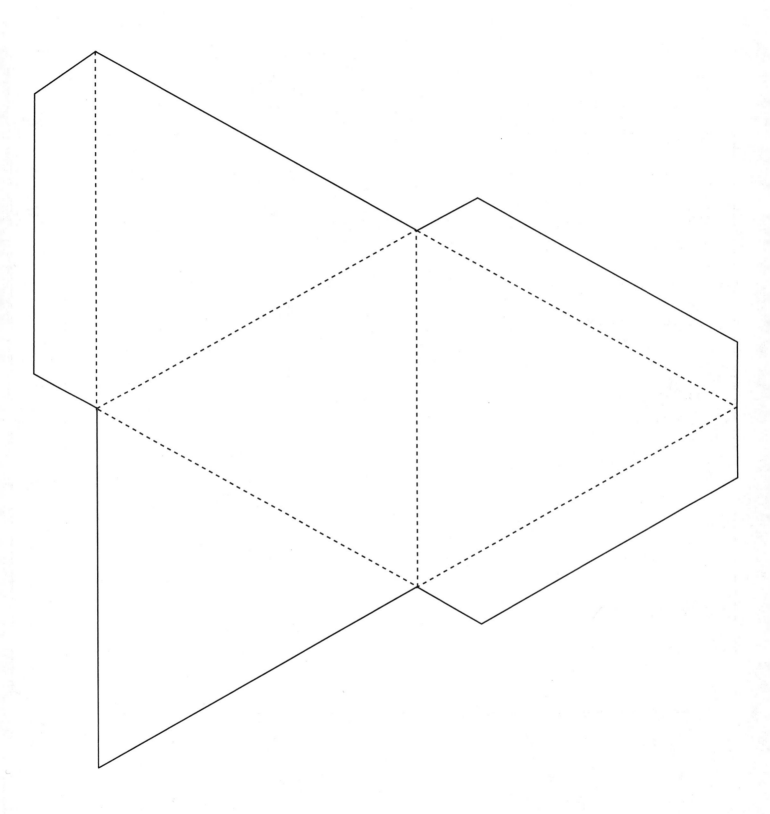

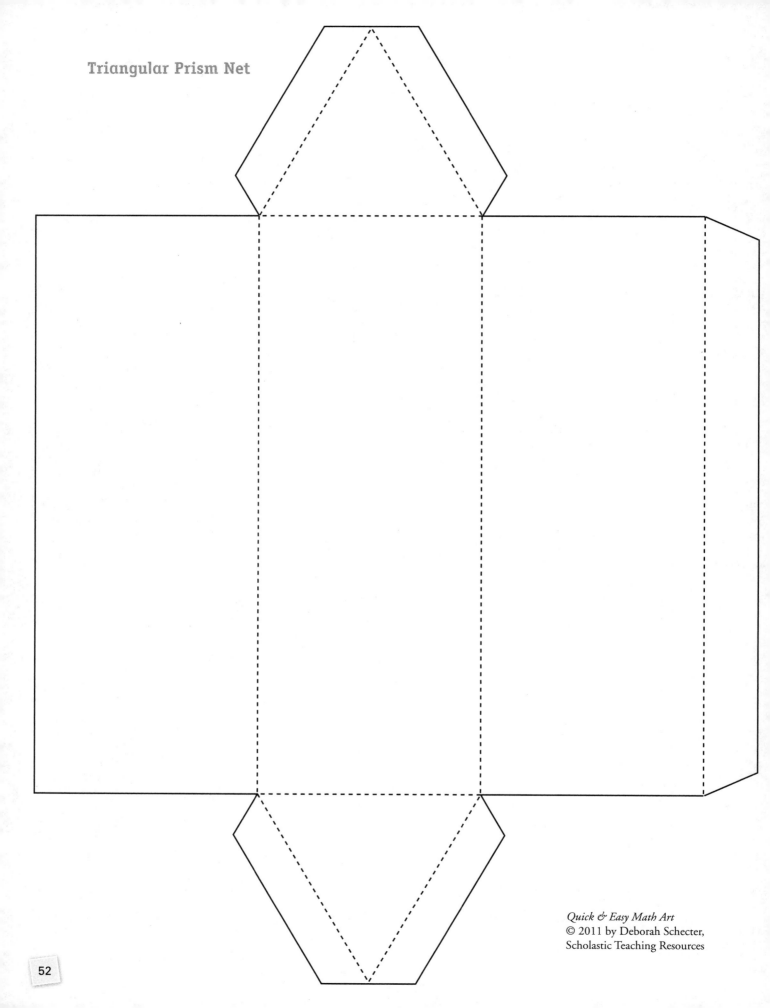

Triangular Prism Net

Quick & Easy Math Art
© 2011 by Deborah Schecter,
Scholastic Teaching Resources

Awesome Origami

As students explore the ancient art of paper folding, they learn about geometric shapes, symmetry, fractions, and more.

Find out what students know about origami. Explain that it is a Japanese word that means "paper folding." Using this ancient art form, they'll be able to transform a single sheet of paper into a colorful ornament or mask they can wear. As students make the folds in each step, ask questions that guide them to focus on the number, size, and type of geometric shapes (squares, rectangles, triangles), fractions (halves, fourths), angles (acute, obtuse, right), and lines of symmetry that emerge. Details and tips for each project follow.

Teaching Tips

❋ Before students begin, model how to make each project using a large paper square.

❋ Paper that is colored or patterned on one side and white on the other, such as wrapping paper, works well.

❋ Have students work on a hard, flat surface and use a fingernail or a ruler to make sharp creases.

❋ When a project is complete, you might have students unfold the paper and observe the shapes and patterns they created.

Ornament-in-the-Round

Materials

❋ student directions, page 55

❋ 6- or 8-inch thin paper squares in contrasting colors (foil gift wrap works especially well)

❋ glue sticks or tape

❋ yarn or ribbon

● You might have a group of students work together for this project, with each student creating one or two of the folded triangle shapes that will become part of the final ornament.

(*continued*)

- In step 8, to make it easier to slide the flaps of one triangle into the pockets of another, tell students to gently squeeze the pockets open. Or use a finger to pry them open a bit.

- Have students use a bit of tape to secure the triangles together; or dab some glue inside each of the pockets.

- Punch a hole in one of the points on the finished ornament and hang with yarn or ribbon.

Bedazzling Bird Mask

Materials

- student directions, page 56
- 16-inch paper squares (bulletin board paper works well)
- scissors
- hole punch
- 16-inch lengths of string or yarn, two for each mask
- crayons, colored pencils, or markers
- craft glue
- craft materials (scrap paper, craft feathers, glitter glue)

- In step 5, to add dimension to the beak, have students fold the mask back along the middle crease, unfold, and then lift up the beak again.

- Assist students in cutting holes for eyes (step 6).

- Encourage students to use symmetry when decorating their masks, making each side a mirror image of the other.

Ornament-in-the-Round

1. Fold a paper square in half from side to side. Then unfold.

2. Fold the square in half the other way. Then unfold.

3. Fold in all four corners to the middle. Crease well.

4. Fold the bottom corner to the top, making a triangle.

5. Fold one top corner down to the bottom edge.

6. Fold the triangle in half away from you, making a smaller triangle.

7. Repeat steps 1–6 to make 7 more folded triangles.

8. Put your ornament together: Slide the flaps of one triangle into the pockets of another. Continue, connecting all of the triangles to form a closed wreath.

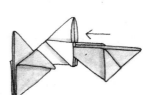 

Bedazzling Bird Mask

1. Fold a paper square in half on the diagonal, then unfold. Fold in the two sides so they meet in the middle.

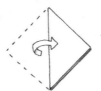

2. Fold down the wide top corner.

3. Fold up the narrow bottom corner to meet the top edge.

4. Fold down part of the narrow corner. This is the bird's beak.

5. Lift up the beak so it sticks out.

6. Cut holes for eyes.

7. Punch a hole on each side. Tie on string.

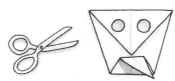

8. Decorate your mask! Use crayons, scrap paper, glitter glue, feathers, and more.

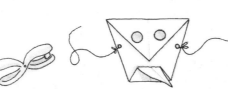

Painting With Perspective

Students investigate perspective by drawing lines to create "3-D" scenes.

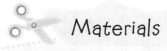 Materials

* copy paper
* pencils
* rulers
* crayons, colored
  pencils, or markers

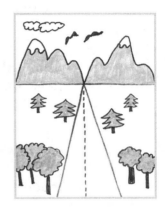

1. Show students examples of pictures that create the illusion of depth, for example, Van Gogh's painting, "Bedroom in Arles." (www.vangoghgallery.com/catalog/Painting/715/Vincent_s-Bedroom-in-Arles.html) Discuss how the artist used perspective to create a three-dimensional effect on a two-dimensional canvas. Then give students paper, pencils, and rulers and have them follow these steps:

To create a room:

* Place your paper in a horizontal position. Use a ruler to draw a rectangle in the center of the paper.

* Draw diagonal lines from corner to corner that intersect in the center of the paper.

* Erase the X shape inside the center rectangle.

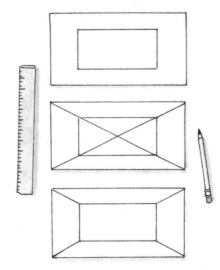

Teaching Tip

As students draw, ask: "What shapes do you see?" (*triangles and trapezoids*) Also help them to notice perpendicular lines and right, acute, and obtuse angles.

2. Guide students to notice that the lines they drew created the illusion of a ceiling, floor, and walls. Invite students to color and decorate their rooms.

To create a scene with a horizon:

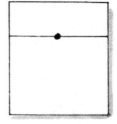

- Place your paper in a vertical position. Use a ruler to draw a horizontal line across the paper about a third of the way down from the top.

- Make a dot in the center of the line. (The dot is a guide and can be erased later.)

- From the black dot, draw two lines toward the bottom of the paper, forming a tall triangle.

- Draw a dashed line down the center of the triangle.

3. Discuss how the lines students drew created the effect of a road that seems to disappear on the horizon. Have them add details to their picture, such as mountains, trees, or skyscrapers. Guide them to draw larger objects in the foreground and smaller ones in the background to enhance the illusion of distance.

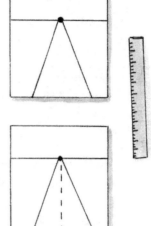

Explore More

❋ When drawing rooms, encourage students to experiment with the size of the rectangles they draw. They'll discover that smaller rectangles make the rooms they draw appear deeper.

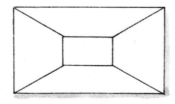

❋ When drawing a scene with a horizon, have students experiment with drawing more than one triangle in different places on the paper to create different effects.

Connect-the-Dot Graph Art

Students practice coordinate graphing by plotting ordered pairs to reveal mystery pictures.

Materials

- coordinate pairs lists, page 60
- 1-cm grid paper, page 61
- pencils
- rulers
- crayons, colored pencils, or markers

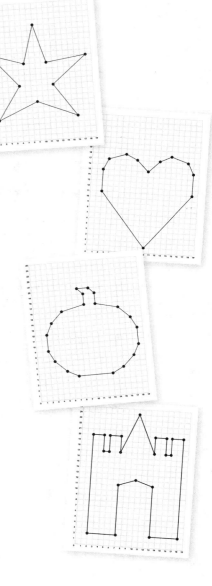

1. Introduce or review coordinate graphing. Copy a sheet of grid paper onto transparency film for use on an overhead or scan for an interactive whiteboard. Model how to find and mark a point on the graph using an ordered pair. Then plot a second ordered pair, and use a straightedge to connect the two points.

2. Demonstrate how to create a simple picture, such as the outline of a house, by plotting a set of six ordered pairs as follows: (4,5), (4,14), (10,20), (16,14), (16,5), (4,5). Then connect the dots in the same order as you made them.

3. Give students a copy of the coordinate pairs list page and sheets of grid paper. Have them plot and connect points (in the order they make them) to see a mystery picture emerge. Then invite students to color and add details to their graph art pictures using crayons or markers.

Explore More

Challenge students to create connect-the-dot pictures for classmates to solve. They first sketch a simple picture on grid paper, then record the list of ordered pairs needed to make it. Students then swap lists with a classmate and plot each other's pictures.

Coordinate Pairs Lists

---

1. (2, 4)
2. (6, 10)
3. (1, 16)
4. (7, 14)
5. (9, 21)
6. (11, 14)
7. (18, 15)
8. (12, 10)
9. (16, 4)
10. (9, 7)
11. (2, 4)

---

1. (10, 1)
2. (2, 11)
3. (2, 15)
4. (3, 17)
5. (6, 18)
6. (8, 17)
7. (10, 15)
8. (12, 17)
9. (14, 18)
10. (17, 17)
11. (18, 15)
12. (18, 11)
13. (10, 1)

---

1. (10, 20)
2. (11, 19)
3. (11, 17)
4. (15, 16)
5. (17, 14)
6. (18, 12)
7. (18, 9)
8. (17, 7)
9. (15, 5)
10. (13, 4)
11. (7, 4)
12. (5, 5)
13. (3, 7)
14. (2, 9)
15. (2, 12)
16. (3, 14)
17. (5, 16)
18. (9, 17)
19. (9, 19)
20. (8, 20)
21. (10, 20)

---

1. (2, 2)
2. (2, 20)
3. (4, 20)
4. (4, 17)
5. (5, 17)
6. (5, 20)
7. (7, 20)
8. (7, 17)
9. (10, 24)
10. (13, 17)
11. (13, 20)
12. (15, 20)
13. (15, 17)
14. (16, 17)
15. (16, 20)
16. (18, 20)
17. (18, 2)
18. (13, 2)
19. (13, 11)
20. (10, 12)
21. (7, 11)
22. (7, 2)
23. (2, 2)

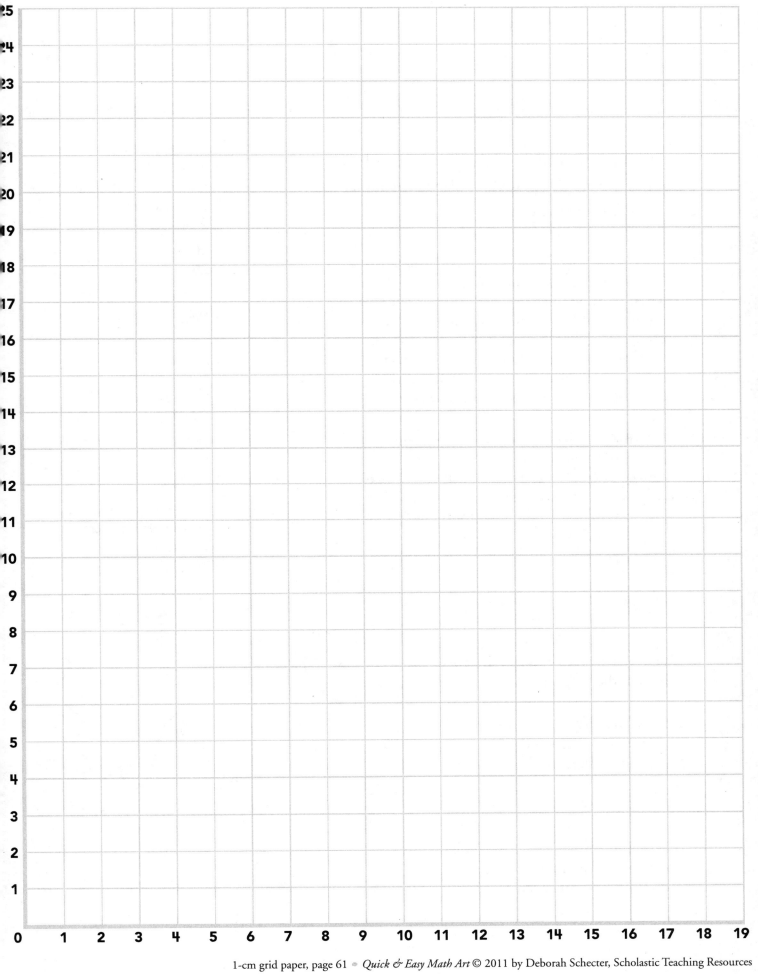

Symmetry Circus

By folding and cutting paper in different ways students create symmetrical circus animals, acrobats, and clowns.

1. Review the concept of symmetry. Explain that a line of symmetry divides a shape into identical parts. In some cases, as with a heart shape, there is one line of symmetry. In other cases, there is more than one, as with a snowflake. Show students examples of symmetrical and non-symmetrical objects or pictures and ask them to identify the ones that contain symmetry.

2. Tell students that they are going to make symmetrical circus animals, performers, and clowns by folding and cutting paper in different ways. Let students choose from the following projects and model the steps for them.

Materials

* symmetrical and non-symmetrical objects or pictures (rocks, scalene triangles, leaves, hearts, snowflakes)

* heavyweight construction paper

* clown pattern, page 63 (copied or glued on cardstock)

* $8\frac{1}{2}$-inch squares of copy paper

* tape

* pencils

* scissors

* crayons, colored pencils, or markers

* craft glue

* craft materials (wiggle eyes, pompoms, pipe cleaners, yarn, paper scraps)

Animal Standups

1. Fold a sheet of construction paper in half, the long way.

2. Draw the outline of half of a simple animal along the fold, cut it out, then unfold.

3. Fold down the head.

4. Add features using coloring tools, wiggle eyes, pompoms, pipe cleaners, and paper scraps.

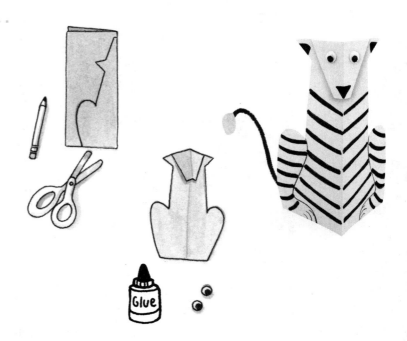

Aerial Acrobats

1. Fold a sheet of construction paper in half, the short way.

2. Draw the outline of an acrobat along the fold, then cut it out, and unfold.

3. Decorate and hang using yarn or string.

Circle of Clowns

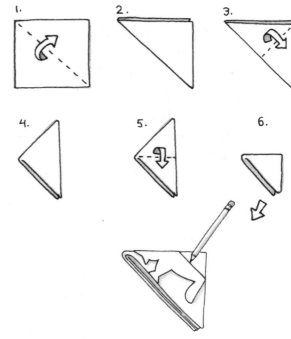

1. Fold an $8\frac{1}{2}$-inch square of copy paper in half on the diagonal. Crease well. Then fold it in half on the diagonal two more times. Crease well.

2. Use a bubble of tape to attach the half-clown pattern to the folded triangle along the thick folded side. Trace and cut it out through all layers of the paper, then unfold. Remove the pattern.

3. Decorate and glue to a construction paper background, if desired. How many lines of symmetry do you see? *(four)*

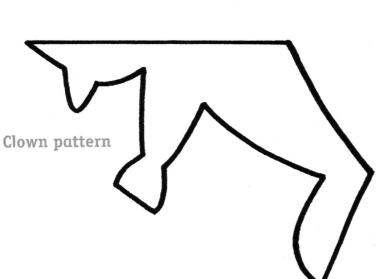

Clown pattern

Paper Shape Transformations

Students explore transformations by using reflections, rotations, partitions, and translations to create beautiful cut paper designs.

✂ **Materials**

* 6-inch and 3-inch construction paper squares
* 12-inch construction paper squares in a contrasting color
* 6- by 9-inch construction paper sheets
* pencils
* scissors
* glue sticks

Reflections

1. Introduce the concept of reflection (flips) by cutting a piece from each side of a paper square and flipping it to create a mirror image. Point out to students that nothing is added or taken away. Then tell students that they are going to create geometric designs using reflection.

2. Give each student a 6-inch paper square, a larger square to serve as a background, pencils, scissors, and glue sticks. Then have students follow these steps:

- Draw different shapes (geometric or abstract) around the edge of the small square, leaving space between each one. (The shapes should not overlap.)

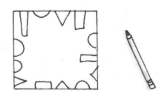

- Cut out the shapes and set them aside. Then center and glue the cutout square on the larger square.

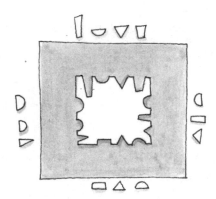

- Flip each small paper shape and place it opposite its matching opening in the square.

- Check that each small shape touches the edges of the square and creates a mirror images of its opening. Then glue the shapes in place.

3. Display students' designs and discuss the effect of negative and positive space created by using reflection.

Rotations (Turns)

Have students repeat the activity but instead of placing the cutout shapes directly opposite their openings in the square, they rotate the shapes around a point on the square. Then they can glue the design to a larger sheet of paper.

Partitions

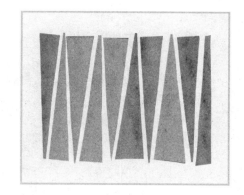

Have students cut a paper square or another shape into a series of pieces (thin strips, triangles, arches, angles). Then they separate and arrange the pieces (in the same order as they were cut) to recreate the original shape. Have them glue the design to a larger sheet of paper.

Translations (Slides)

Using this technique, students slide an object from one position to another. Give each student three 3-inch paper squares and a 6- by 9-inch sheet in a contrasting color, and then have students follow these steps:

- Fold each small square in half, draw a shape on the folded edge and then cut it out.

- Place the first cutout square frame (negative space) in the top left hand corner of the large sheet of paper.

- Next to it, place the object that was cut out (positive space).

- Continue with the remaining cut squares, alternating positive and negative pieces. Then glue them in place.

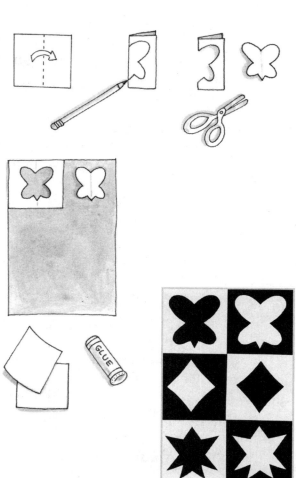

Tessellation Ties

Students use transformations to create tessellated patterns on ties they can wear.

Materials

* pattern blocks or cut paper shapes
* tie pattern, page 69 (enlarge, if desired)
* tessellation patterns, page 70
* glue sticks
* cardboard
* scissors
* pencils
* crayons, colored pencils, or markers
* hole punch
* notebook reinforcements
* 24-inch lengths of yarn or string

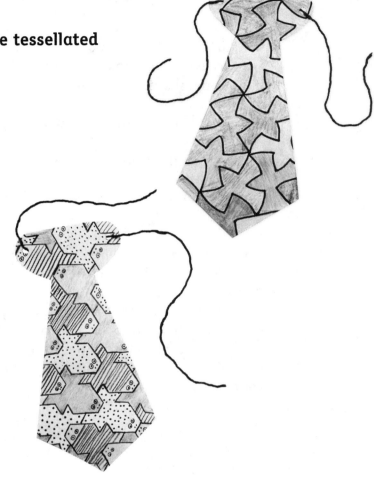

1. Begin by introducing or reviewing tessellations. Explain that a tessellation is a design made of shapes that fit together like a puzzle and repeat over and over in a pattern. Discuss and point out examples of tessellations, such as in tiled floors and brickwork, and in patterns on clothing, ceilings, roofs, wallpaper, quilts, and honeycombs.

2. Explain to students that sliding or rotating shapes from one position to another can make a tessellation. Squares, rectangles, hexagons, rhombuses, and some triangles are examples of shapes that tessellate. Have students use pattern blocks or paper shapes to identify shapes that do and do not tessellate.

Teaching Tip

Ancient Islamic art, medieval stained glass windows, and American folk art, such as quilts, use tessellations. Visit the following Web sites to show students examples of the works of M.C. Escher, an artist famous for using tessellations.

* **The Oldest Escher Collection on the Web**

  mcescher.net

* **Totally Tessellated**

  library.thinkquest.org/16661/

3. Give each student a copy of the tie and tessellation pattern pages, cardboard, glue sticks, pencils, and scissors. Then have students follow these steps:

- Cut out the tessellation pattern block you wish to use. Glue it to cardboard, and then cut out the shape.

- Place the shape on your tie pattern. Trace it. Then slide or rotate the shape in any direction so it fits together with the one you just traced.

- Continue sliding and tracing your shape to cover the tie.

- Use colored pencils or markers to color and draw designs on the tessellated pattern.

- Cut out your tie. Punch two holes as shown. (Stick notebook reinforcements on the backs of the holes.) Then thread the yarn through the holes. Ask your teacher to help you tie on your tie!

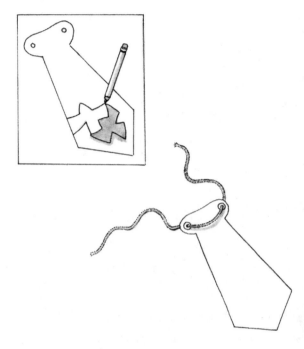

Explore More

✻ Students might also create tessellated designs on other shapes such as eggs, fish, butterflies, or turtles.

✻ Invite students to try making their own tessellation patterns.

1. Cut a simple shape, such as a square, out of cardboard.

2. Cut a piece out of one side.

3. Slide the cutout piece to the other side of the shape, so that it lines up exactly with the cutout on the opposite side. Tape it in place.

4. Repeat steps 2 and 3 on the other sides of the square, if desired.

5. Trace and slide the cardboard shape as described above.

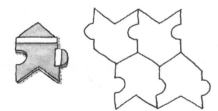

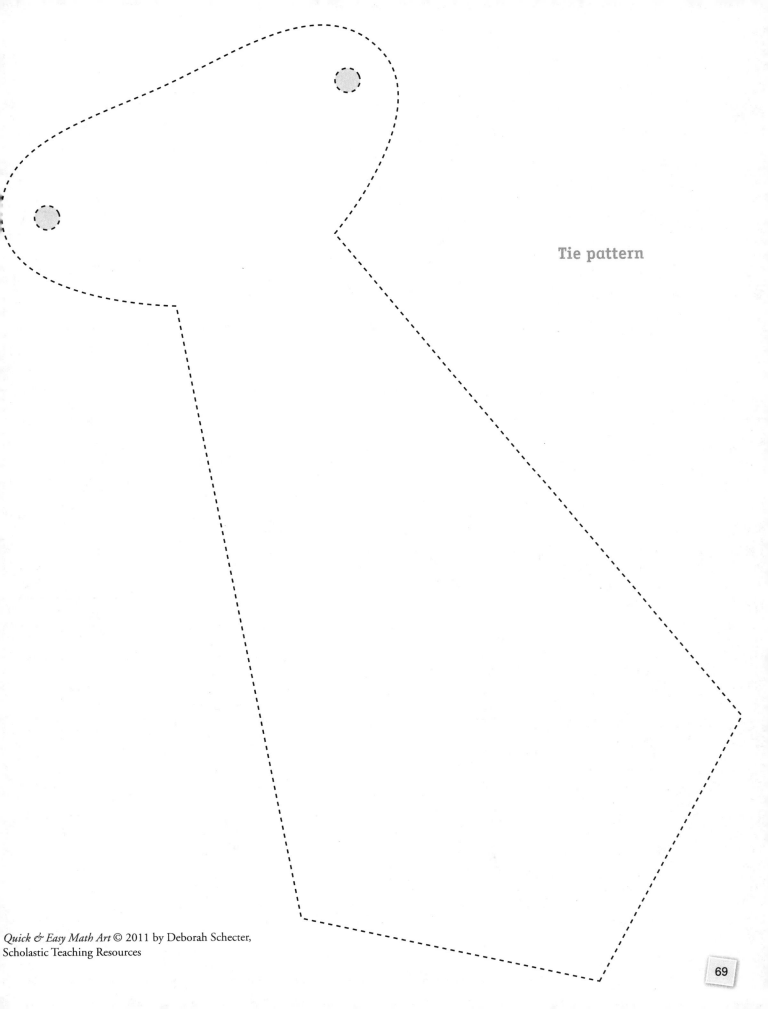

Tie pattern

Tessellation patterns

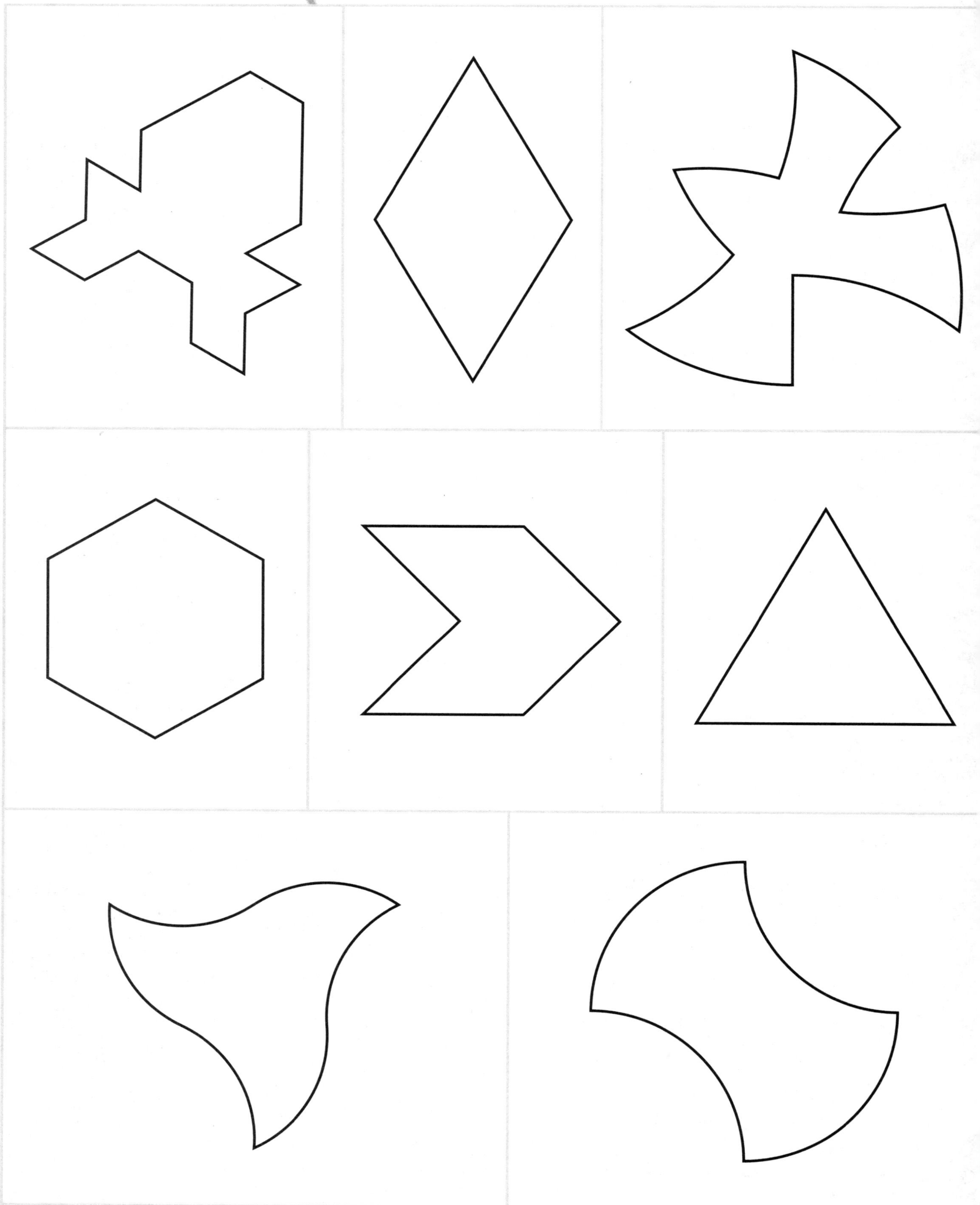

Rainbow Bead Rulers

Enliven measurement practice by inviting students to make their own colorful rulers using beads.

1. Give each student a pony bead and a ruler. Tell students to place the bead on their desk so that the holes are on each side. Ask them to estimate the width of the bead and then use a ruler to measure. (*A pony bead is exactly $\frac{1}{4}$-inch wide.*) Ask: "How many beads would you need to measure one inch?" (*4*) "How many would you need to measure 6 inches?" (*24*) Tell students that they are going to make their own colorful 6-inch rulers using pony beads.

2. Divide the class into small groups. Provide each group with a bowl of pony beads. Give each student two pipe cleaners, a paper plate, and a copy of the chart. Then have students follow these steps:

   - Count 24 beads and place them on your plate. For each group of four, choose the same color, and then alternate or use contrasting colors for the other groups.

   - Starting at one end, twist the two pipe cleaners together to create a three-inch section. Bend to form that section into a loop. Then, holding the two pipe cleaners together, string the beads on them in groups of four, alternating colors to demarcate each inch.

   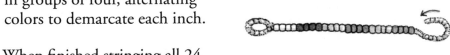

   - When finished stringing all 24 beads, push the beads together tightly, and twist the remaining section of the two pipe cleaners together and form a loop.

   - Estimate the length of each item on the chart and record your estimate. Then use your ruler to measure it. Use the $\frac{1}{4}$-inch bead increments to measure to the nearest quarter-inch. Add other items to your chart and estimate and measure them, too.

Materials

For each ruler:

❋ two 12-inch pipe cleaners

❋ ruler

❋ 24 pony beads, assorted colors

❋ paper plate

❋ Measurement Chart, page 72

Teaching Tips

❋ Students can use a fine-tip permanent marker to record the inches on their ruler by numbering every fourth bead, if desired.

❋ For accuracy, tell students to hold the loop at each end of their ruler and gently pull the ruler taut when measuring.

Measurement Chart

What I Measured	Estimate	Actual Measurement
crayon	_____ inches	_____ inches
glue stick	_____ inches	_____ inches
large paper clip	_____ inches	_____ inches
CD case	_____ inches	_____ inches
_____	_____ inches	_____ inches
_____	_____ inches	_____ inches
_____	_____ inches	_____ inches

Snaky Tape Measures

These handy tape measures give students practice measuring in metric and customary units—and then fold up to fit in their back pockets!

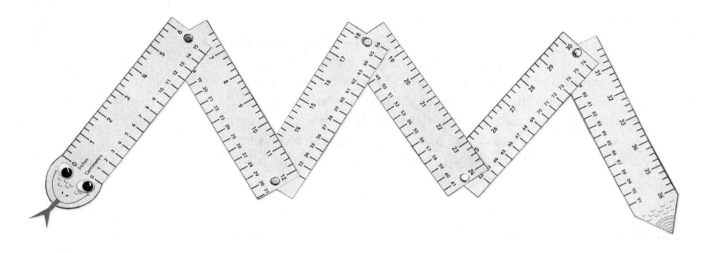

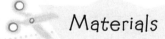

Materials

For each tape measure:

* Snaky Tape Measure patterns, page 75

* lightweight cardboard (recycled file folders work well)

* glue stick

* hole punch

* notebook reinforcements

* 5 brass fasteners

* crayons, colored pencils, or markers

* craft materials (wiggle eyes, paper scraps)

* Measure Me Chart, page 76

1. Give each student a copy of the pattern page. Then have students follow these steps to make their tape measures:

* Glue the page to lightweight cardboard, then cut out the strips.

* Punch holes in the strips as indicated and stick notebook reinforcements on the backs of the holes.

* Assemble the tape measure. Line up the strips in numerical order. Then use a brass fastener to connect the end of each strip to the beginning of the next. (The strips should overlap—left over right.) Color and decorate your snake.

2. Pair up students to practice measuring with their Snaky Tape Measures. Ask them to measure the distance from the floor to the top of their desks first in centimeters and then in inches. Remind them to align the "0" with their desktop. Show them how they can fold back the excess part of the tape measure when they reach the floor. Have students check each other's measurements.

3. Give each student a copy of the Measure Me Chart. Students continue to work in pairs to first estimate and record—in centimeters and inches—the length of each of their body parts named on the chart (and any others they would like to add). To check their estimates, they take turns measuring each other using their Snaky Tape Measures. Discuss strategies for rounding up or down to the nearest centimeter or inch when an object falls between increments.

4. Once the groups have finished measuring, have them compare their estimates with their results. Discuss strategies students used to take measurements that were greater than the length of their tapes, for example, their height.

Explore More

Have students order or graph their measurement results from longest to shortest.

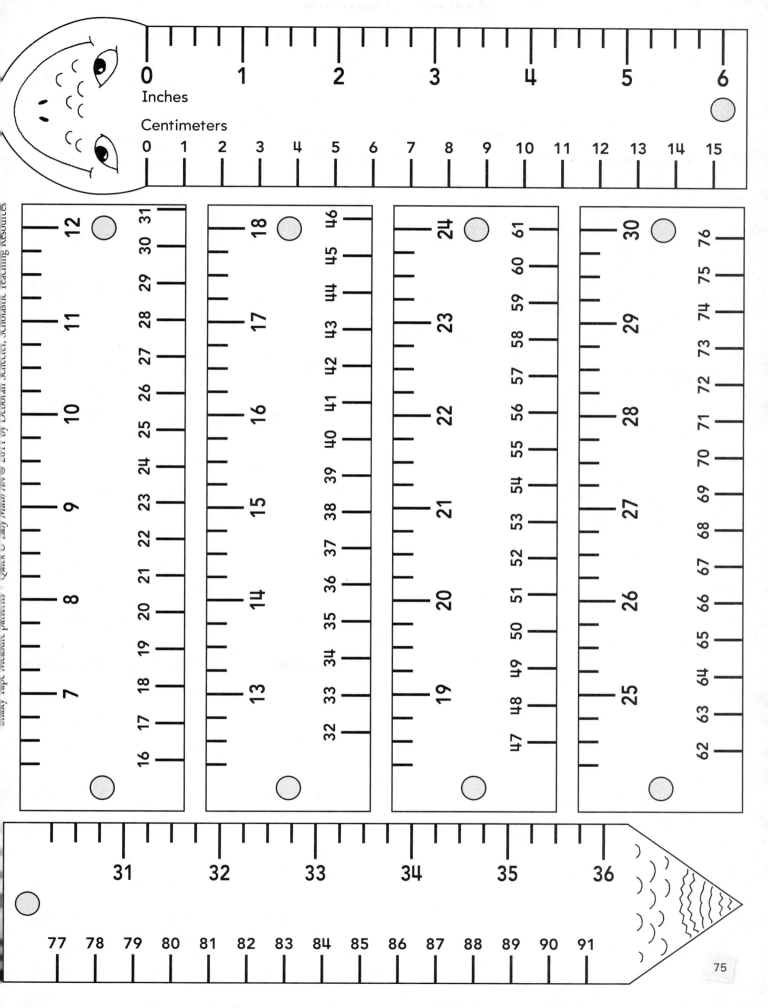

0 1 2 3 4 5 6
Inches

Centimeters
0 1 2 3 4 5 6 7 8 9 10 11 12 13 14 15

75

Measure Me Chart

What I Measured	Estimate	Actual Measurement
my height	_____ inches _____ centimeters	_____ inches _____ centimeters
my arm	_____ inches _____ centimeters	_____ inches _____ centimeters
my leg	_____ inches _____ centimeters	_____ inches _____ centimeters
_____	_____ inches _____ centimeters	_____ inches _____ centimeters
_____	_____ inches _____ centimeters	_____ inches _____ centimeters
_____	_____ inches _____ centimeters	_____ inches _____ centimeters

Quick & Easy Math Art © 2011 by Deborah Schecter, Scholastic Teaching Resource

Metric Strip Sculptures

Students practice measuring in metric to create sculptures made from paper strips.

Materials

- 9- by 12-inch heavyweight construction paper
- metric rulers or Snaky Tape Measures, page 75
- pencils
- scissors
- glue sticks
- tape
- cardboard or old file folders, cut in half

1. Tell students that they are going to sculpt with paper strips that they will measure and cut. Review with students the centimeter units on their rulers, then give each student a sheet of construction paper. Also provide pencils, scissors, glue sticks, and tape.

2. Direct students to measure and cut 11 strips from a sheet of paper. Each strip should be 2 centimeters wide but a different length. The first strip should be 30 centimeters long and each successive strip should be 2 centimeters shorter (28 cm, 26 cm, 24 cm, and so on). The last strip should be 10 centimeters long.

3. Invite students to use the strips to create three-dimensional sculptures. They might change the shape of the strips by making pleats, folding zigzags, curling, or fringing, and then glue or tape the ends to a cardboard base. Or they might experiment making closed geometric shapes that fit one inside the other. Students could turn these into animal forms or abstract mobiles.

4. When the projects are completed, create a display and invite the class to compare and contrast the ways students shaped the different lengths of paper strips in their sculptures.

Teaching Tip

To keep track of the lengths, have students calculate and then write the length of each strip on scrap paper before measuring and cutting.

Perfect Pocket Pouches

Students practice their measurement skills to make a handy pouch to take wherever they go.

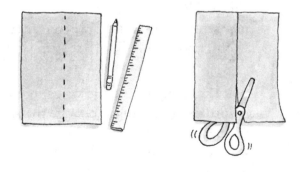

✂ Materials

For each pouch:

❄ 9- by 12-inch piece of light-colored felt (makes 2 pouches)

❄ ruler

❄ pencil

❄ scissors

❄ stapler

❄ brass fastener

❄ craft materials (felt scraps, fabric glue, fabric paint, markers, glitter glue, yarn, ribbon)

Give each pair of students a 9- by 12-inch piece of felt, a ruler, pencil, and scissors. Then have students follow these directions to make their pouches.

1. Measure $4\frac{1}{2}$ inches in from one long edge of the felt. Use a pencil to mark the measurements along the length of the felt and then use the ruler to connect the markings with a straight line. Cut the felt in half along the line. You and your partner each take one half of the felt.

2. Measure and fold the felt $4\frac{1}{2}$ inches up from the short end.

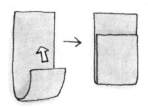

3. Staple the sides closed to make a pocket, and then gently turn the pocket inside out.

4. Round the corners of the top flap using scissors. Then fold down the flap.

5. Use the point of a sharp pencil to make a tiny hole in the center of the flap and through to the front of the pocket, directly underneath.

6. From inside the pocket, poke the prongs of a brass fastener through both holes. To close the pouch, bend down the prongs of the fastener. Then decorate your pouch.

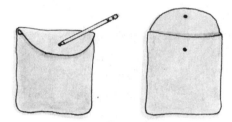
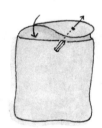

7. Optional: To wear the pouch, measure and cut a 36-inch length of thick yarn or ribbon. Then unfasten the flap and lay the yarn or ribbon above the pocket. Refasten and tie around the waist.

Angle Art

Students use acute, right, and obtuse angles to create artful angle pictures.

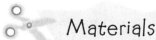

Materials

- Angle Tester pattern, page 81
- plastic straws
- pipe cleaners
- scissors
- toothpicks
- craft sticks

- construction paper (for a background)
- crayons, colored pencils, or markers
- craft glue
- craft materials (paper scraps, yarn, glitter glue, wiggle eyes)

obtuse

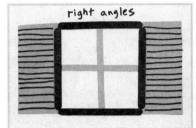

acute angle

acute

acute

obtuse

right angles

1. Review the different kinds of angles with students. Explain that angles are formed where two straight lines meet at a point. Ask students to hold out their arm and bend their elbow to show first an acute angle, then a right angle, and finally an obtuse angle. Then ask students to look around the room and identify different angles in objects they see (for example, *angles formed by the hands on a clock, corners on books, chairs, and tables*).

2. Give each student a copy of the Angle Tester, a straw, a pipe cleaner, and scissors. Demonstrate how to use these items to measure angles:

   - Insert the pipe cleaner in the straw and trim off the excess.
   - Bend the straw to match the angle on the item or picture being measured.
   - Place the bent straw on the Angle Tester to determine whether it is an acute, right, or obtuse angle.
   - Straighten the straw to measure each new angle.

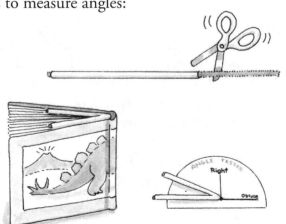

3. Have students make a three-column chart, such as the one shown here, to record the types of angles they find.

acute	right	obtuse
number 7	window frame	clock hands at 10:15

4. Tell students that they are to create pictures that include different angles. For example, they might depict a bird's beak using an acute angle; a kite might include both acute and obtuse angles.

5. Provide students with straws, pipe cleaners, toothpicks, and craft sticks to use in forming angles, and a sheet of construction paper. Have students glue one or more of their angles to the paper (trimming pipe cleaners and straws, as needed), and then use coloring tools and craft materials to create the rest of the picture.

6. Students can then swap papers and use their Angle Testers to measure the angle(s) in the pictures. Each artist then labels his or her picture with the angle(s) used.

Angle Art Collages

Let students go on an angle scavenger hunt to find pictures to use in a collage.

* Provide old magazines and catalogs and invite students to search for pictures to cut out that show each of the three types of angles.

* Have students use their Angle Tester and straw device to measure and then group the angles by type. Then they glue each group to a sheet of paper or oaktag and label.

* Make an "Artful Angles" bulletin board display with students' collages. Discuss the different angles students found and ask questions, such as: "Do some kinds of angles in the pictures appear more often than others? Which pictures have the most unusual examples of angles?"

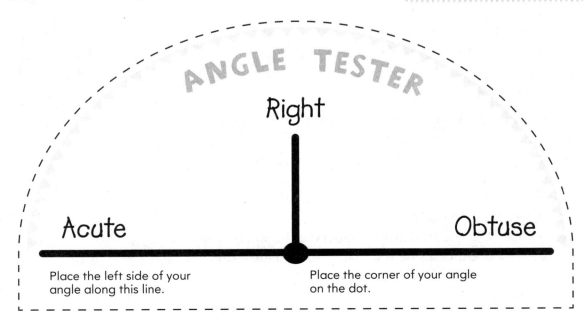

ANGLE TESTER

Right

Acute

Obtuse

Place the left side of your angle along this line.

Place the corner of your angle on the dot.

Area and Perimeter Pals

Students explore perimeter and area as they create creatures on grid paper.

Materials

- 1-cm grid paper, page 61
- pencils
- crayons, colored pencils, or markers
- construction paper
- glue sticks
- craft materials (wiggle eyes, feathers, glitter glue)

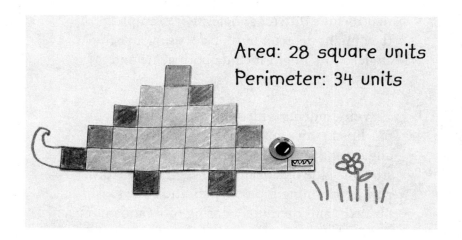

Area: 28 square units
Perimeter: 34 units

1. Ahead of time, color six squares on a sheet of grid paper to form a rectangle.

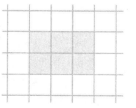

Teaching Tip

Mask the numbers on the grid paper before photocopying, if desired.

2. Use the shape to review perimeter and area with students. Ask: "What is the perimeter of this rectangle?" (*10 units*) Explain that the perimeter of the rectangle is the distance (or number of units) around the outside of a shape. To find the perimeter, students should count the sides of the units. Then ask students to determine the area of the rectangle. (*6 square units*) Guide students to understand that the area is the number of units inside the shape. To find area, they count the number of whole (square) units.

3. Give each student a sheet of grid paper. Invite students to explore shading squares on the grid in pencil to create a creature—real or imaginary.

4. Give them a fresh sheet on which they can copy their picture using coloring tools.

5. Have students work with partners to determine the perimeter and area of their creatures.

6. Students can then cut out their creatures, glue them to a sheet of construction paper, and add decorative details. Have students record the area and perimeter of their creature on the paper. Showcase students' creations in a display titled "Area and Perimeter Pals."

Explore More

Can creatures have the same area but different perimeters? Encourage students to draw different figures or shapes using 20 or 30 squares, for example. How many different configurations can they come up with?

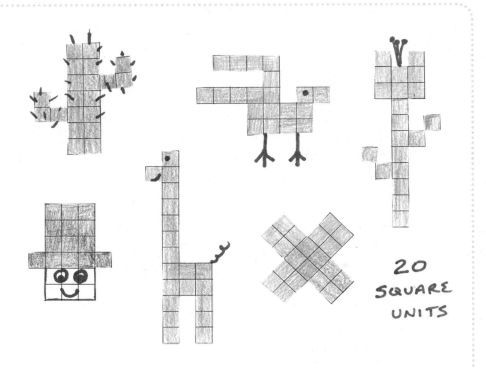

20 SQUARE UNITS

Ghoulish Gloves

How much can these creepy hands hold? Students hone their estimation skills and explore volume to find out!

1. Ahead of time, fill a glove with beans (up to about an inch from the opening) and use a twist tie to close. Show students the filled glove and a bean. Have them estimate how many beans the glove holds and record their estimates on a sheet of paper.

2. Divide the class into groups. Give each group a glove and a bag of beans. Have students count out the number of beans in their estimates and begin filling the glove.

3. When it is half-filled, or if students have used all of the beans in their estimates before it is half-filled, ask them if they want to revise their estimates. If so, have them record the new figure. Ask: "How did you decide on your new estimate?"

4. Have students finish filling the glove using the number of beans from their revised estimates, if they made a revision. Tell them to loosely fill—not stuff—the glove up to about one inch from the opening. (Have them return any extra beans to the bag. Then give each group a twist tie to close the glove.)

5. Recruit volunteers to count the number of beans in the sample glove you prepared. As a class, compare students' individual estimates with the actual results. Ask students to describe their estimating methods. Were their revised estimates more accurate?

6. Set up a center where students can paint glow-in-the-dark hand bones on their gloves. Allow the paint to dry. Then darken the room and get ready for a fun-filled fright!

Materials

For each glove:

* disposable latex glove (small size)
* dried kidney beans (about 2 cups)
* zip-closing plastic bag
* ruler
* twist tie
* glow-in-the-dark paint (the type that comes with a fine-tip applicator)

Explore More

Repeat the activity using uncooked rice and $\frac{1}{4}$ measuring cups or tablespoons instead of dried beans. Have students estimate how many measures of rice will be needed to fill the gloves.

Starry Constellation Clocks

These cool, glow-in-the-dark clocks give students a fun way to practice telling time.

Materials

- clock face and hand patterns, below, and page 86 (copied onto cardstock or glued to cardboard)
- scissors
- hole punch

- glow-in-the-dark paint (the type that comes with a fine-tip applicator)
- brass fasteners

Optional:
- craft glue
- glow-in-the-dark glitter

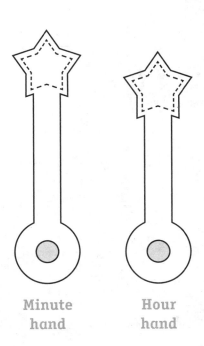

1. Have students follow these directions to make their clocks.

   - Cut out the clock and hands. Use a sharp pencil to poke a hole in the dot on the clock face, then punch a hole in the circle on each hand.

   - Paint the numbers on the clock face, the hands, the surrounding stars, and other night sky details.

   - Attach the hands to the clock (minute hand on top of the hour hand) using a brass fastener.

   - Dot glue around the clock face and sprinkle with glitter, if desired.

2. At different times of the day, dim the lights and call out the time. Students then set their clocks. To see if they set their clocks correctly, turn on the lights and have students check the classroom clock.

Minute hand   Hour hand

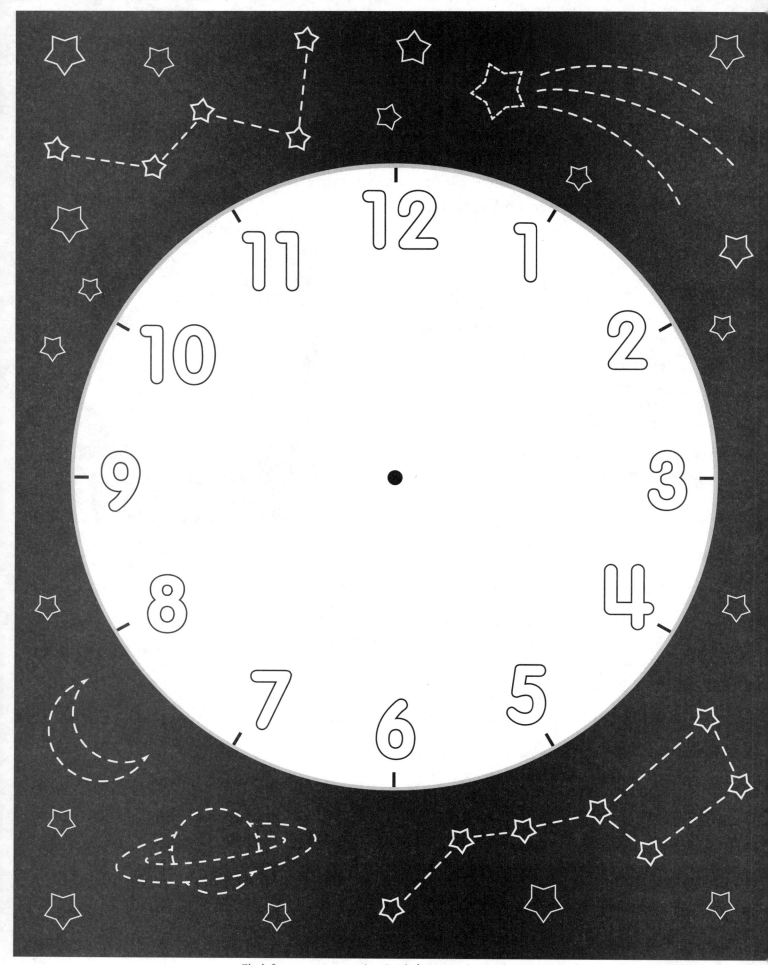

• *Quick & Easy Math Art* © 2011 by Deborah Schecter, Scholastic Teaching Resource

Cupcake Combinations

Introduce students to the study of combinations by inviting them to create delectable, designer cupcakes!

✂ Materials

❋ cupcake patterns, page 90

❋ crayons, colored pencils, or markers

❋ large sheets of construction paper (for "tray" background)

❋ glue sticks and craft glue

❋ craft materials (construction paper scraps, confetti, glitter glue, sequins)

© CUPCAKE CAFÉ ©
FLAVORS: Vanilla, Chocolate
ICINGS: White, Green, Pink
Designs: Stripes, Dots
2 x 3 x 2 = 12

1. Begin by asking students to name their favorite kinds of cupcakes. What flavor cupcake do they like best? Icing? Toppings? List students' responses (for example, *chocolate cake, pink icing, colored sprinkles*; *yellow cake, chocolate icing, no sprinkles*). Discuss the fact that different preferences mean different combinations. Then tell students that they will pretend to be bakers, and their job will be to "bake" cupcakes that come in a variety of combinations.

2. Copy the cupcake pattern page onto transparency film for use on an overhead or scan for whiteboard use. (Have an extra copy available for use in step 3.) List different flavor and icing possibilities:

cupcake flavor: vanilla or chocolate   **icing:** white, pink, green

Ask "How many different cupcake combinations can we make with these cupcake flavor and icing choices?" Allow students plenty of thinking time, then invite them to share their ideas and explain their reasoning. Color the cupcakes to illustrate students' responses. (There are six possible combinations.)

3. Have students study the results. Then ask, "How can we be sure that we did not repeat any combinations and that we found all of them?" Encourage students to share a pattern or strategy that could be used to determine all of the options, for example, drawing sketches or making lists. (See Using a Tree Diagram, page 89, for more.)

4. Divide the class into pairs or small groups and give each several copies of the cupcake pattern page. Invite them to design a tray of cupcakes, each of which has a different combination of ingredients. Variations might include: cake flavor, icing flavor, icing designs (stripes, zigzags, squiggles), toppings (sprinkles, dragées, "candy" hearts, shamrocks, flowers). Students can create their variations on cupcake cutouts using craft items and coloring tools. To complete their projects, have them glue the cupcakes to a large tray shape cut from construction paper.

5. Make a "Cupcake Café" display of students' cupcake combinations. Encourage students to share the strategies they used to come up with their combinations. Then invite students to pick out their favorites!

To keep the activity from getting too complicated, you might have students limit their choices, for example, two cupcake flavors, two icing colors, and two or three icing designs.

Explore More

Continue your combination investigations throughout the year by inviting students to use construction paper and craft items to design different combinations of decorated valentine hearts, spring butterflies, Halloween monster masks, or holiday snowflakes.

Using a Tree Diagram

You might want to introduce students to a tree diagram— a tool for helping them determining all possible combinations. You might also show them how to use multiplication to find the number of cupcake combinations (and check their tree diagrams):

Cupcake Combinations in Step 2
(page 87)

cake flavor   icing

cupcake

vanilla
- white
- pink
- green

chocolate
- white
- pink
- green

2 cupcake flavors x 3 icings = 6 combinations

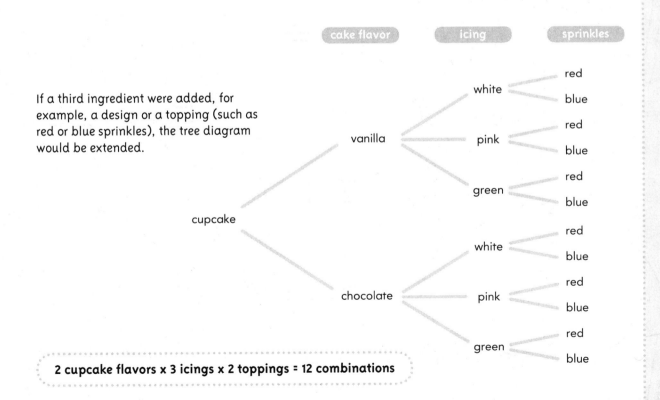

If a third ingredient were added, for example, a design or a topping (such as red or blue sprinkles), the tree diagram would be extended.

cake flavor   icing   sprinkles

cupcake

vanilla
- white — red, blue
- pink — red, blue
- green — red, blue

chocolate
- white — red, blue
- pink — red, blue
- green — red, blue

2 cupcake flavors x 3 icings x 2 toppings = 12 combinations

Cupcake patterns

Leafy Venn Collages

Students use a Venn diagram to sort and classify leaves and create collages from nature.

✂ Materials

- plastic bags
- assorted leaves (see Teaching Tips, below)
- telephone books
- heavy books
- paper towels
- oaktag or posterboard
- craft glue
- yarn
- scissors
- field guide to leaves (optional)

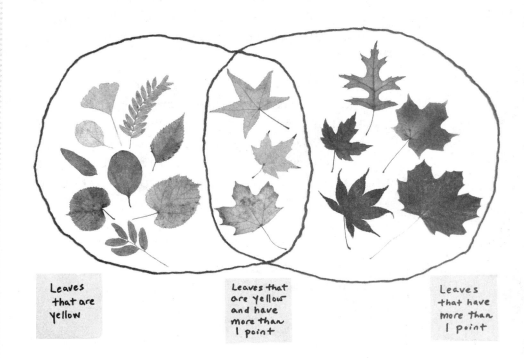

Leaves that are Yellow

Leaves that are yellow and have more than 1 point

Leaves that have more than 1 point

1. Give each student a plastic bag and take a leaf-collecting walk. Encourage students to look carefully at the shapes, colors, sizes, and textures of the leaves they see and to collect as many different types as they can.

2. Back in class, help students place the leaves they've collected between the pages of thick telephone books, first placing the leaves between paper towels to absorb excess moisture. Put several heavy books on top. In about two or three weeks, the leaves will be dry and flat.

Teaching Tips

- If you live in an area where leaves turn colors and fall off trees in autumn, this is a perfect time to plan this activity. (But check for possible allergies beforehand.)

- Reinforce respect for living things by discussing reasons for picking up leaves from the ground rather than taking them off trees.

3. Spread out the leaves and invite students to identify ways to sort them by attributes such as color, size, shape (number of lobes, edge type, broad-leaf or needle-like, vein pattern). Use a field guide to leaves for reference.

4. Have students work individually or in pairs to choose 10 to 15 leaves, sort them into two groups, then think about which leaves share attributes of both groups. Have students move those leaves together to create a third group.

5. Provide yarn, scissors, glue, and large sheets of construction paper. Show students how to use the yarn to create an overlapping Venn diagram to glue to their paper. Then have them glue their leaves, according to attribute groupings, inside the appropriate sections of the circles.

6. Display students' leafy Venn diagram collages. Invite classmates to guess the sorting rules used in each. Students can then add labels to their projects that describe their groups.

Teaching Tip

Instead of using yarn, students can draw their Venn diagrams using markers.

Sand Castle Glyphs

Students collect and display information about themselves by making sand castle glyphs.

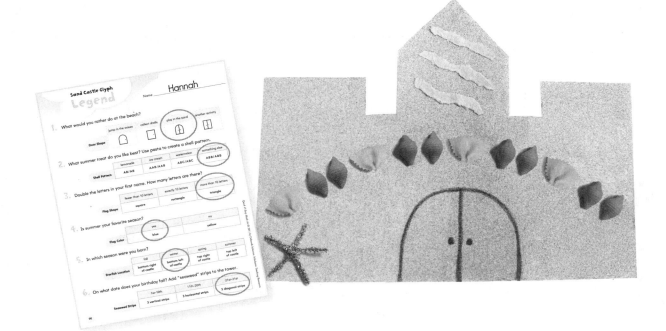

 ## Materials

- Sand Castle Glyph Legend, page 96
- sand castle pattern, inside back cover (glued to cardboard)
- sandpaper
- dried pasta (small shell, bow tie, cone-shaped campanelle)
- craft glue

- gold, yellow, or orange pipe cleaners, cut into quarters
- scissors
- paper scraps
- crayons or markers
- construction paper (for a background)
- toothpicks

1. Ahead of time, make several sand castle patterns for students to share. Then use the legend and craft materials to make a glyph that describes you and your preferences. Also copy the legend onto transparency film for use on an overhead or scan for whiteboard use.

2. Introduce or review glyphs with students. Explain that a glyph conveys information about data that has been collected in the form of a picture. Show students your completed sand castle glyph and explain that the details on the sand castle tell information about you. Have students look at the legend and see if they can figure out what your sand castle glyph tells about you. Discuss what each element on the legend represents. Then tell students that they are going to make their own sand castle glyphs.

3. Give each student a copy of the legend, the sand castle pattern, and a sheet of sandpaper. Have students trace the pattern on the sandpaper, and then cut out the sand castle.

4. Students circle or mark their preference for each of the six questions on the legend. Then they use the craft materials to decorate their sand castle to reflect these preferences. When complete, they mount their glyph on construction paper.

5. Display students' completed glyphs with a copy of the legend. Then invite students to interpret each glyph and tell what they learn about each glyph's owner. You might also have students summarize the information in a written description.

Teaching Tips

❋ Break bowtie pasta in half to create shapes that resemble fan-shaped shells. Students can paint the pasta "shells," if desired.

❋ To make a starfish, students twist together two quarter-size pieces of a pipe cleaner, and then wrap a third piece around the center to form the fifth point. Trim ends, if needed.

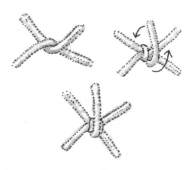

❋ Have students cut out and color flag shapes from white scrap paper and tear "seaweed" strips from green paper.

❋ For their flagpoles, students can either glue a toothpick to the top of their castle or draw a line.

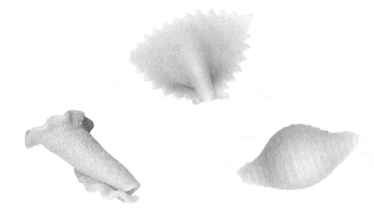

Turn Glyphs Into Graphs

Extend the activity by using the information on the glyphs to make graphs. For example, you can graph the beach activities, or the summer treats, by the number of students that prefer each one. Ask questions, such as:

- Which beach activity do students in our class like best? Least?
- Do more students prefer collecting shells or jumping in the waves?
- How many more students would rather jump in the waves than collect shells?

Wearable Glyphs

At the beginning of the school year, invite students to make glyph bracelets or necklaces to share information about themselves and get to know one another.

- Make copies of the legend below or create and customize your own.

- Provide students with beads in different colors (or dyed tubular pasta) and lengths of yarn.

- Students use the legend to show information about themselves by stringing the corresponding color and number of beads (if applicable) on a length of yarn. They can string the beads in any order or pattern they wish.

- Invite students to tie on their beaded creations and roam the room with a copy of the legend to learn about their classmates.

☆ ☆ ☆ Legend ☆ ☆ ☆	
Yellow	boy
Orange	girl
White	how old you are (Add the number of beads equal to your age.)
Blue	have brother(s) or sister(s) (1) have both (2)
Black	have a pet (1) don't have a pet (2)
Red	went to this school last year (1) went to a different school last year (2)
Green	like to read fiction best (1) like to read nonfiction best (2)

Sand Castle Glyph
Legend

Name _____

1. What would you rather do at the beach?

	jump in the waves	collect shells	play in the sand	another activity
Door Shape				

2. What summer treat do you like best? Use pasta to create a shell pattern.

	lemonade	ice cream	watermelon	something else
Shell Pattern	AB/AB	AAB/AAB	ABC/ABC	ABB/ABB

3. Double the letters in your first name. How many letters are there?

	fewer than 10 letters	exactly 10 letters	more than 10 letters
Flag Shape	square	rectangle	triangle

4. Is summer your favorite season?

	yes	no
Flag Color	blue	yellow

5. In which season were you born?

	fall	winter	spring	summer
Starfish Location	bottom right of castle	bottom left of castle	top right of castle	top left of castle

6. On what date does your birthday fall? Add "seaweed" strips to the tower.

	1st–10th	11th–20th	21st–31st
Seaweed Strips	3 vertical strips	3 horizontal strips	3 diagonal strips